Six Sigma
for Managers

Other titles in the Briefcase Books series include:

To learn more about titles in the Briefcase Books series go to
www.briefcasebooks.com

Six Sigma
for Managers

Second Edition

Greg Brue

New York Chicago San Francisco Athens
London Madrid Mexico City Milan New Delhi
Singapore Sydney Toronto

1 2 3 4 5 6 7 8 9 0 DOC/DOC 1 2 0 9 8 7 6 5

ISBN   978-0-07-183863-4
MHID   0-07-183863-5

e-ISBN   978-0-07-183864-1
e-MHID   0-07-183864-3

This is a CWL Publishing Enterprises book developed for McGraw-Hill Education by CWL Publishing Enterprises, Inc., Madison, Wisconsin, www.cwlpub.com.

Dedicated to Lauren Brue
for her unwavering support of my professional life.
This book was better because of you.
Thank you, my love!

Contents

Foreword

O ver the last few decades, it has been my distinct privilege to serve as Greg Brue's Six Sigma mentor. I have closely watched him extend and perfect his base of knowledge during the '90s, as evidenced by the increasing depth and scope of his many Black Belt projects. Owing to this solid technical foundation, others began to seek his advice and leadership.

During the early '90s, Greg focused his pursuit of Six Sigma by leveraging his leadership skills on the issues surrounding implementation and deployment over the course of his tenure at the Six Sigma Academy. Moving into the 21st century, Greg rightfully positioned himself as a true global leader on the playing field of Six Sigma. Today, he is forging new and original ideas from the solid ore mined from his past, as evidenced in this book.

Mikel J. Harry, Ph.D.
Founder and CEO
Six Sigma Academy

Preface

ix Sigma is best described as a journey—a journey for business professionals who are truly committed to improving productivity and profitability. Six Sigma isn't theoretical; it's an active, hands-on practice that gets results. In short, you don't *contemplate* Six Sigma; you *do* it. And doing it has proven to be the fast track to vastly improving the bottom line. The journey is about arming your human "assets" with problem-solving techniques, working project by project, resulting in breakthrough financial benefits and defect reduction.

The purpose of this new edition of *Manager's Guide to Six Sigma* has been to update and capture both the evolution of Six Sigma from the onset of the methodology back in 1994 with AlliedSignal/GE through the then-new revolution of the "big data business analytic." The techniques have been enhanced, and the body of knowledge is even more powerful now as it's developed in this data rich environment.

The Six Sigma story began in the 1980s at Motorola, where it was first developed and proven. In 1983, reliability engineer Bill Smith concluded that if a defect was found in a product and corrected during production, then it might be that other defects were being missed and found later by customers. In other words, process failure rates were much higher than indicated by final product tests. His point? If products were assembled completely free of defects, they probably wouldn't fail customers later. This is when Six Sigma took off and the methodology was continuously refined to not only eliminate process waste, but also turn it into growth currency—regardless of the type of service, product, or market sector. The rest, as they say, is history.

Six Sigma statistically measures and reflects true process capability, correlating to such characteristics as defects per unit and probabilities of success or failure. Its value is in transforming cultural outlooks from complacency to accomplishment across the gamut of industries.

Most companies function at 4 sigma—tolerating 6,210 defects per one million opportunities. Operating at 6 sigma creates an almost defect-free environment, allowing only 3.4 defects per one million opportunities: products and services are nearly perfect (99.9997%). Eliminating defects eliminates waste and defects within a process and greatly enhances customer satisfaction.

Of course, this sounds good in theory, but how do you put it into practice? Well, Six Sigma is about arming your employees with the training, resources, leadership support system, and knowledge to solve problems and reach nearly defect-free production. It's also about taking a leadership journey to guide these human assets toward ever-increasing achievement. Six Sigma asks hard questions about your processes and gets the data to answer these questions. It provides solutions that fit your unique processes.

That's why I refreshed the content this book—I want to share updated Six Sigma real case stories to show how to achieve greater growth and improved customer service. Intense, results-driven, and ultimately exciting, Six Sigma eliminates wasteful variation, changes business cultures, and creates the infrastructure you need to initiate and sustain greater productivity, profitability, and customer satisfaction. In the following pages, you'll find out *what, why,* and *how* Six Sigma works so you can start on your own Six Sigma journey. This book is designed for business leaders who want to know the reality of Six Sigma and who are ready for major breakthroughs to improve their companies' bottom-line profits.

Some of the material used in this book comes from my book *The McGraw-Hill 36-Hour Course in Six Sigma,* which provides even more specific details about the Six Sigma DMAIC breakthrough strategy.

Chapter Highlights

In Chapters 1 and 2, you'll learn the basics; it's an introduction to Six Sigma and why you should put it into practice. You'll find an introduction to the breakthrough strategy phases of Define, Measure, Analyze, Improve, and Control. There's a review of how to define quality as well as how to measure performance. I'll show how Six Sigma makes you more competitive at every level—from streamlining internal processes to improving your external market position. You'll also learn how to engage employees as you transform cost into growth.

Building on this base, in Chapter 3 I share a practical, realistic proven strategy for implementing Six Sigma. The focus is on kicking off your Six Sigma initiative. The text provides the essential steps, tips, and planning guidelines you need to get it right. By properly readying your organization, you can lay the best foundation for a successful implementation of Six Sigma. Everyone has a role to play, from executives to line workers.

Chapters 4 through 8 are the heart of the Six Sigma methodology and go into great detail on the breakthrough strategy of DMAIC: Define is Chapter 4, Measure is Chapter 5, Analyze is Chapter 6, Improve is Chapter 7, and finally, Control is Chapter 8. Each chapter goes through goals and objectives for each phase and the tools and techniques, with updated case studies to show the practical application as you take the journey through the Six Sigma strategy to solving business problems.

Chapter 9 then takes you into how to sustain Six Sigma and shows you how to keep the momentum going to realize an ever-increasing return on investment. This is where knowledge transfer happens: as you and your teams transform theory into practice and become experts in the methodology, you'll share the strategies that create an extraordinary ripple effect throughout the organization.

As you delve into Chapter 10, you'll have the opportunity to review real case studies and final reports about Six Sigma projects. The object of this chapter is to further demonstrate that Six Sigma is not a passing quality fad, but rather, a real-world business tool that returns positive financial results across the business spectrum. The evidence of its success is found in the proven results achieved by the companies profiled here.

I want to also thank all the thousands of Green Belts, Black Belts, and MBBs alongside the executives and champions supporting the unending journey of Six Sigma. This book could not have been as real without the true stories of these real people doing the heavy lifting during journey. Thank you!

Special Features

Titles in the Briefcase Books series are designed to give you practical information written in a friendly, person-to-person style. The chapters deal with tactical issues and include lots of examples. They also feature numerous sidebars that give you different types of specific information. Here's a description of the sidebars you'll find in this book.

KEY TERM
The Key Term sidebars provide definitions of terms and concepts as they're introduced. Because Six Sigma has a lot of new terminology, you will find many of these sidebars.

SMART

MANAGING
The Smart Managing sidebars do just what their name suggests: give you tips to intelligently apply the strategies and tactics described in this book to help you implement the principles that we explain.

TRICKS OF THE TRADE
Tricks of the Trade sidebars give you insider how-to hints that astute managers use to execute the techniques described in this book.

FOR EXAMPLE
It's always useful to have examples that show how the principles in the book are applied. The For Example sidebars provide illustrations of how managers can use the these ideas.

CAUTION
Caution sidebars warn you where things could go wrong when undertaking a Six Sigma initiative.

How can you make sure you won't make a mistake when you're trying to implement the techniques the book describes? You can't, but the Mistake Proofing sidebars give you practical advice on how to minimize the risk of this happening.

TOOLS

The Tools sidebars provide specific directions for implementing the techniques described in the book in a systematic fashion.

Introduction to Six Sigma

Knowledge is power.
                    —Francis Bacon (1561–1626)

The assertion that knowledge is power is as true now as it was four centuries ago. In any industry, in any organization, for any process, when you don't know what you don't know, it's going to cost you. For too many organizations, the costs (often hidden) of defects and waste in the way they operate are huge. Occasional errors in processes may not seem like such a big deal. But when you consider how many errors may be lurking in processes throughout an organization, the monetary impact can be staggering.

Six Sigma generates knowledge. It can reveal errors, defects, and wastes in the operations of any organization. The power of knowledge increases, often dramatically, through action taken with Six Sigma to reduce errors, defects, and waste.

What Is Six Sigma?

Six Sigma is a methodology for using a set of techniques and tools to improve product or service quality by identifying and reducing or eliminating the causes of defects or errors and minimizing variability in processes. People within the organization are trained to apply the techniques and tools in improvement projects, in which teams set measura-

Six Sigma Methodology for using a set of techniques and tools to **KEY TERM** improve product or service quality by identifying and reducing or eliminating the causes of defects or errors and minimizing variability in processes.

ble goals (e.g., reduce process cycle time by 7%, increase sales by 5%, reduce costs by 8%) and follow a specific sequence of steps.

The name of this methodology, Six Sigma, comes from the statistical concept of sigma. We discuss sigma in the next section.

Evolution of the Six Sigma Fundamentals

Whatever you read about Six Sigma will probably state that it was developed in 1986 by Motorola and that it's a set of techniques and tools. Both of these statements are true, but not the whole truth. Actually, Six Sigma is a methodology based on thinking that can be traced back for several millennia and on applying fundamentals with which most people are at least somewhat familiar.

We all know about Socrates (469/470–399 BCE), the Greek philosopher considered the father of Western philosophy. Among other things, Socrates is known for an approach to learning that consists of asking a series of questions to not only elicit answers but, more generally, to encourage thinking—the Socratic method. The Socratic method asks questions and follows up the answers with more questions, eventually leading to an answer that withstands further questioning.

The Socratic method led to the development of the scientific method, which begins with a *hypothesis* (a proposed explanation for an observable occurrence such as a problem) and which is tested for accuracy. The *Oxford English Dictionary* defines the

Hypothesis Proposed explanation for an observable occurrence, such as a **KEY TERM** problem. A hypothesis is nothing more than a suggested answer to a question, an answer that leads to eliciting ideas and collecting data to prove or disprove the hypothesis.

scientific method as "a method or procedure that has characterized natural science since the 17th century, consisting in systematic observation, measurement, and experiment, and the formulation, testing, and

TEST YOUR HYPOTHESES WITH DATA
In Six Sigma, a hypothesis must always be tested with data.
There is no "I believe" or "I think" or "I feel." What we believe,   **CAUTION**
what we think, and how we feel may help us form a hypothesis,
but only facts matter in proving or disproving it. In applying Six
Sigma, we do not deviate from this path. We can arrive at a hypothesis in
any way we choose, but we must prove or disprove that hypothesis with
data and statistical analysis.

modification of hypotheses."

The scientific method of identifying causes of problems and using critical thinking to solve them is fundamental to Six Sigma. In fact, Six Sigma could be described as a methodology that uses the scientific method with statistical tools.

Further evolution of Six Sigma can be linked to Carl Friedrich Gauss (1777–1855), considered one of the most influential mathematicians in history. Gauss introduced the concept of the normal curve, or normal distribution, also known as the Gaussian distribution or Gaussian curve. If we do something again and again, we can expect the results to start to show a pattern, to form what is known as a normal distribution or, because of its shape, a bell curve (Figure 1-1). The normal distribution underlies the statistical assumptions of the Six Sigma model. It is the basis for analytical or inferential statistics, which are used to establish the capability of a process.

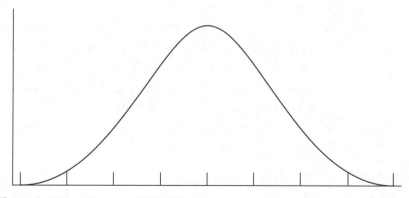

Figure 1-1. Simple normal distribution curve

What Is Sigma?

As mentioned earlier, the Six Sigma methodology was named for the statistical concept of sigma. *Sigma* (represented by the Greek letter σ) is a term that represents *standard deviation*, which is a measure of variation in a product or a process. *Variation*—the deviation from the expected or the ideal—is what causes defects. Standard deviation helps us understand how far a process deviates from a reference of perfection. (We get into calculating the standard deviation in later chapters.) The lower the standard deviation, the closer the data points tend to be to the mean.

KEY TERMS

Sigma Statistical term that represents standard deviation, a measure of variation in a product or a process. In Six Sigma, sigma is used to measure a process in terms of the number of defects and the number of opportunities for defects. This ratio of defects to opportunities is generally expressed as defects per million opportunities (DPMO).

Defect Measurable characteristic of the process or its output outside of acceptable customer limits, i.e., not conforming to specifications.

Opportunity Point in a value-added process where a defect could result or where the product or service fails to meet customer requirements, specifications, or expectations.

Use of DPMO and sigma level enables us to compare processes throughout an organization, whatever the nature of the processes and however the terms *defect* and *opportunity* are defined specifically for each of those processes.

A sigma represents 691,462.5 defects per million opportunities, which translates to a percentage of nondefective outputs of 30.854%. That's obviously really poor performance. If we have processes functioning at a three sigma level, this means we're allowing 66,807.2 defects per million opportunities, or delivering 93.319% nondefective outputs. That's much better, but we're still wasting money and disappointing our customers 6.681% of the time. Figure 1-2 shows different levels of sigma.

Six Sigma as the Goal

When Motorola developed the Six Sigma methodology in 1986, it set a goal of six sigma for its manufacturing operations. If a process is operat-

1 sigma = 691,462 DPMO
2 sigma = 308,538 DPMO
3 sigma = 66,807 DPMO
4 sigma = 6,210 DPMO
5 sigma = 233 DPMO
6 sigma = 3.4 DPMO

Figure 1-2. Sigma levels and probabilities of defects per million opportunities (DPMO)

ing at the level of six sigma, we can expect 99.99966% of its outputs to be free of defects. In other words, it's working nearly perfectly. Six sigma is a statistical concept that measures a process in terms of defects. Achieving a performance level of six sigma would mean that your processes are delivering only 3.4 defects per million opportunities (DPMO).

COST OF QUALITY AT MOTOROLA

Here's a blunt reality: In 1987, Motorola discovered that poor quality accounted for approximately 25% of its annual inventory carrying costs. Since this expense added no value, it was like taking $250 million and burning it ... annually. Another fact that came out of the Motorola discovery period was that the highest-quality producer was the lowest-cost producer. The synergy is that simply by improving quality, you can decrease costs and reduce cycle time—and increase customer satisfaction.

How well are your processes operating? Are they at three sigma? At four sigma?

Most organizations in the U.S. are operating at quality levels between three and four sigma. That means they could be losing up to 25 percent of their total revenue due to processes that deliver too many defects—defects that take time and effort to repair and that create unhappy cus-

DEVIATE AN INCH, LOSE A THOUSAND MILES

As this Chinese proverb states, even a small deviation in a process can have big consequences. Deviation, variation, defect, waste—whatever you call it, the result is the same: It costs you! Whatever your business—manufacturing, distribution, or other services—any variation and the resulting defects are hurting your bottom line.

tomers. Is that good enough? The answer is simple: No, not when you could be doing a lot better.

The central idea of Six Sigma management is that if you can measure the defects in a process, you can systematically find ways to eliminate them, to approach a quality level of zero defects.

Sigma Level: An Example

Let's take an example, an all-too-familiar scenario: lost luggage at the airport. Many of us have experienced the frustration of watching the baggage carousel slowly revolve while waiting for luggage that never arrives. The system is far from perfect. But just how far, in sigma measurement terms?

In general terms, the baggage handling capability of many airlines is performing at around the three sigma level. That means there are about 66,000 "defects" for every one million luggage transactions, which equates to approximately a 94% probability that you'll get your luggage.

Is that good enough? Certainly not for the customers whose bags are among the defects. The defects increase airline costs because employees must deal with misplaced luggage and unhappy passengers. And those defects can result in the loss of future business.

If the airline can achieve a six sigma level of performance in luggage handling, it clearly pays off in terms of lower costs and happy passengers, who are then more likely to fly with that airline again.

It may seem like three sigma is good enough. After all, if there are 66,807 defects per million opportunities, that means 933,193 opportunities without a defect—93.319% perfection.

But if the airline is taking comfort in those statistics, it's losing money and losing customers. Consider this three-sigma level from another perspective.

For customers, three sigma represents highly unsatisfactory performance. The airline is not meeting its most basic expectation—that its customers' luggage will be put on the same flight and travel with the customers to the same destination. So the airline is likely to be losing many of those frustrated customers.

Three-sigma performance also costs money. Variations—time, waste, and errors—abound in the baggage-handling process: misrouting the baggage, reporting the problem, processing the report, searching, retrieving, and finally delivering the lost luggage. When you translate the 6% probability gap of missing luggage into monetary terms, the hard cost of this defect can be much higher than 6% of the overall cost of handling luggage—perhaps several million dollars per year. If the baggage-routing process were improved, the margin for error would be reduced and the allocation of resources, both human and monetary, could be more profitably used.

How many customers can your business afford to lose? How much money can your company afford to lose due to mistakes? Why accept it as normal to be running processes at only three sigma or four sigma when, by changing the way you manage your processes, you could get a lot closer to six sigma and all the resulting benefits?

Why not just four sigma? That's the level of quality achieved by many major companies—99.379%. Because that goal is not high enough. It's been calculated that if 99% were good enough, we would be accepting the following:

- Every hour the postal service would lose 20,000 pieces of mail.
- Every day our drinking water would be unsafe for almost 15 minutes.
- Every week there would be 5,000 surgical operations that go wrong in some way.
- Every month we would be without electricity for almost seven hours.

So, is 99% good enough?

Six Sigma uncovers the layers of process variables—in data terms—that you must understand and control to eliminate defects and wasteful costs. It's a management approach that aims to achieve the apex of quality by measuring, analyzing, improving, and controlling processes to root out defects and boost bottom-line results.

Essentials of the Six Sigma Methodology

The Six Sigma methodology uses statistical tools to identify the *vital few factors*, the factors that matter most for improving process quality and generating bottom-line results. These tools are presented and discussed during phases in the Six Sigma process in which they are first used.

There are two forms of Six Sigma: DMAIC and DMADV. DMAIC, the focus of *Six Sigma for Managers*, consists of these five phases:

- **Define.** Determine the project goals and customer (internal and external) deliverables.
- **Measure.** Identify one or more product or service characteristics, map the process, evaluate measurement systems, and estimate baseline capability (the current performance of the process).
- **Analyze.** Evaluate and reduce the variables through graphical analysis and hypothesis testing and identify the vital few factors for process improvement.
- **Improve.** Discover variable relationships among the vital few factors, establish operating tolerances, and validate measurements.
- **Control.** Determine the ability to control the vital few factors and implement process control systems.

We devote a chapter to each of these phases. (Six Sigma DMADV, also known as Design for Six Sigma, consists of these five phases: Define, Measure, Analyze, Design, and Verify.)

Six Sigma focuses on defects and variations. It begins by identifying the critical-to-quality (CTQ) elements of a process—the attributes most important to the customer. It analyzes the capability of the process and aims to stabilize it by reducing or eliminating variations.

The Six Sigma methodology and tools will enable you to identify, correct, and control the CTQ elements and reduce the cost of poor quality (COPQ). (I refer to the COPQ as the "cost of doing it wrong.") Your projects will reveal hidden costs and pinpoint ways to eliminate those costs.

Simply put, Six Sigma management is about tying quality improvement *directly* to financial results. The Six Sigma goal is to link internal processes and systems management to end-consumer requirements.

Six Sigma is a scientific approach to management, driven entirely by data. The Six

SMART **ASK ONE SIMPLE QUESTION**

MANAGING
Try this experiment the next time you're in a meeting and people are discussing a problem. Listen for words such as "I think that this is the real problem" or "I believe this is the solution to the problem." Ask this one simple question: "If that's what you think, what data (facts and evidence) do you have to support your opinion?"

Sigma methodology eliminates the use of opinion—"I think," "I feel," "I believe." Six Sigma drives the organization to a scientific means of decision making by basing everything on measurable data.

ANECDOTAL EVIDENCE
"Anecdotal evidence" is the ultimate oxymoron and an evil source of variation. It's a personal opinion with a sample size of one. Take anecdotal evidence with less than a grain of baby powder.

Focus on Engaging People and Changing Processes

Six Sigma relies on old-fashioned hard work coupled with factual data and a disciplined problem-solving approach. It affects every aspect and level of an organization—from line workers to middle managers to CEOs—to transform your *people* as well as your *processes*.

IT'S NOT ONLY THE PEOPLE
Managers tend to focus only on the people in their organization. When something goes right or something goes wrong, they look for a person to congratulate or to blame. The fact is that work gets done through processes executed by people; both successes and problems are usually the result of what lots of people do, not only one person. If you don't pay careful attention to both people and processes, improvement won't happen.

As the first step in that transformation, the Six Sigma mindset considers you and your people as *resources* (assets), rather than as *costs* (liabilities). That's right—you are as much an asset as any piece of capital equipment and you represent an investment with extraordinary potential for return. Shifting the perspective from people as liabilities to people as assets (or investments) is fundamental to Six Sigma.

Once you're thinking in terms of human assets, it's equally important to realize the underlying monetary value of rooting out wasted materials and steps in processes, as this is key to unlocking the hidden return on your investment in people. And that's also another aspect of the Six Sigma approach to managing.

By changing the way you look at processes, by understanding the vital few factors that cause waste, error, and rework, you can improve the

SMART   **SEE EMPLOYEES AS ASSETS**
MANAGING

SEE EMPLOYEES AS ASSETS
An easy way to understand the concept of human assets is to calculate their individual return on investment (ROI). For example, if an employee costs the business $50,000 a year and his or her activity produces revenue of $100,000, the employee has covered the costs and raised an additional 100%—the profit or ROI. So, the annual ROI for that employee is 100%. By calculating employee ROI, you can focus on making the most of them as assets invested in your business.

ELEVATOR TALK
FOR EXAMPLE
A CEO of a major corporation once asked me, "What's the 30-second elevator speech that explains Six Sigma?" My answer went like this: "Six Sigma is a problem-solving technology that uses your human assets, data, measurements, and statistics to identify the vital few factors to decrease waste and defects while increasing customer satisfaction, profit, and shareholder value."

ability of your processes to deliver higher quality to your customers and to lower costs. Once you know which vital few factors to focus on, you can make improvements that deliver dramatic results.

It's actually simple—once you put your mind to it. By putting your people to work at solving process problems with proven statistical tools, you eliminate not only errors, but also inaccurate speculation about why processes don't work. Instead of opinion, you arm yourself and your people with quantifiable information—based on facts, not hunches and guesswork. When you know the facts, you're in a position to fix the problems permanently and gain long-term benefits. In other words, you've leveraged the power of knowledge to transform performance.

Not Only Statistics, but Cultural Changes

Because it uses statistical terminology, Six Sigma is frequently perceived as a statistics and measurement program. This is not the case. The Six Sigma approach to management uses statistics solely as tools to interpret and clarify data. You focus on tool selection and the use and interpretation of data to drive decisions. Six Sigma practitioners also use computers and statistical software to take advantage of knowledge and to speed the improvement process. The goal is to create Six Sigma companies—companies whose systems and processes are as perfect as possible, functioning at their best performance level.

To achieve that level of quality requires not only statistics, but changes in the organization's culture—the beliefs, expectations, ways of operating, and behaviors that characterize the interactions of the organization's people. Culture evolves over a long time and it often reflects the beliefs and behaviors of top management. Because Six Sigma affects the way things are done, its successful implementation requires a cultural change that may be profound.

The Six Sigma approach is rigorous, requiring from the highest levels of management a deep commitment that permeates the entire organization. It requires a tolerance for endlessly questioning the validity of sacred company beliefs and the traditional ways "things are done around here." It also requires a sense of urgency—an understanding that to solve the problems that undermine profitability and customer satisfaction, you must involve your key people in actively implementing the Six Sigma methodology.

> **Culture** Beliefs, expectations, ways of operating, and behaviors that characterize the interactions of people in any organization. It's "how things are done around here" in an organization.
>
> **KEY TERM**

The Six Sigma approach to management involves cultural change. Essential to this cultural change are key players known as "champions" and "black belts," who act as agents to facilitate that change. Champions and black belts play vital roles in the success of Six Sigma management, as we outline in Chapter 3.

Six Sigma is exciting. But it requires tenacity, mental toughness, and above all, an unwavering dedication to the pursuit of perfection in every aspect of business operations. Once you've fully embraced that, the possibilities are virtually limitless in what you can achieve.

Six Sigma Is *Not* ...

Six Sigma is not another quality program. That's an important point to emphasize.

Businesses exist for one purpose—to profitably serve customers. So it follows that any problem-solving initiative should do the same. Six Sigma uses your resources to fix identifiable, chronic problems. It proves its value by connecting outcomes to your bottom line.

Quality programs lay a valuable foundation in creating a quality mindset. But ask yourself if any of the quality programs you've experienced have generated specific financial results like Six Sigma. It's possible you'll answer no, since a primary criterion for selecting Six Sigma projects is to return money to your balance sheet as the result of *full-time* efforts by dedicated resources.

Six Sigma is not theory. It's a practice of discovering the vital few processes that matter most. It defines, measures, analyzes, improves, and controls these vital processes to tie quality improvement directly to bottom-line results.

Six Sigma is an active, involved effort that puts practical tools to work to root out defects at all levels of your organization. It's not a theoretical exercise: You don't *think* about Six Sigma—you *do* it.

Since the success of Six Sigma is directly linked to monetary outcomes, it generates real-world results. It uses the most readily available resources in an organization—its human assets. That means that positive, tangible results consistently show up wherever and whenever people are engaged in implementing Six Sigma techniques.

CAUTION

SIX SIGMA IS NOT ANOTHER QUALITY PROGRAM

Quality programs are valuable in that they can create a quality perspective and culture. But Six Sigma fixes identifiable, chronic problems that directly impact your bottom line. Six Sigma projects are selected to reduce or eliminate waste, which translates into real money.

Six Sigma is not a training program. Of course, practitioners are trained in the methodology to ensure correct implementations and results. But Six Sigma is a business strategy that fosters a cultural shift at all levels. Permeating departments, functional groups, and all levels of management, Six Sigma changes the outlook and practices of everyone in the organization.

From workers on assembly lines and bookkeepers in accounting to

---

SIX SIGMA MYTHS

SMART

MANAGING

There are many myths and misunderstandings about Six Sigma, notably these:

- It works only in manufacturing settings.
- It doesn't include customer requirements.
- It's repackaged TQM.
- It uses difficult-to-understand statistics.
- It's an accounting game without real savings.
- It's just training.
- It's a "magic pill" with little effort.

Just remember that Six Sigma actively links people, processes, and outcomes in a rigorous yet adaptable way to produce tangible results, whatever the industry, business, product, or service.

---

operations managers and human resource personnel, training exists only to instill the method, facilitate transformation, and get financial results by attacking chronic defects with proven statistical tools.

Six Sigma works because it focuses fanatical attention on the details that matter. The Six Sigma method has worked through several recessions and still holds true to adding breakthrough value. Former GE CEO Jack Welch, who achieved great success with Six Sigma, made the case for Six Sigma succinctly:

> The big myth is that Six Sigma is about quality control and statistics. It is that—but it is a helluva lot more. Ultimately, it drives leadership to be better by providing tools to think through tough issues. At Six Sigma's core is an idea that can turn a company inside out, focusing the organization outward on the customer.... It finally gives us a route to get to the control function, the hardest thing to do in a corporation.

Manager's Checklist for Chapter 1

☑ Six sigma is the optimum level of quality for organizations, averaging 3.4 defects per million opportunities. It can be applied to any transaction in any business.

☑ The Six Sigma methodology and tools will help your organization reduce variations, defects, and waste from all business processes and generate significant financial results.

✓ Six Sigma is a disciplined, five-phase problem-solving methodology for improving processes and effecting culture change by establishing a system for spreading knowledge throughout the organization.

✓ Six Sigma starts with top leadership at the CEO level and it continues with top-level support.

Defining Quality and Measuring Performance

Quality is never an accident; it is always the result of high intention, sincere effort, intelligent direction and skillful execution; it represents the wise choice of many alternatives.

—attributed to John Ruskin (1819–1900)

M any managers operate their organizations by idealistic generalizations—that is, they accept and communicate certain statements they believe to be true about their operations. However, when they are pressed to objectively justify their belief in these axioms and to explain how axioms provide appropriate guidance, they're often at a loss.

They may say, "We are committed to quality" or "We are always improving what we do." But what does "quality" mean? How does it translate into objectives and action? How do you quantify improvement?

With Six Sigma, you measure the extent to which your goods and services meet customer expectations. That's the basic criterion for quality. These are the questions we need to answer:

- What do the customers want?
- What do the customers not want?
- What are you doing to deliver products and/or services that meet your customers' critical-to-quality (CTQ) expectations?
  - What processes are involved in meeting the CTQ expectations?
  - What's happening in those processes?

■ How well are you doing what you're doing?

Start with Your Customers

Six Sigma starts with the customer. It may not be true that the customer is always right, but it's true that it's your customers who essentially define "quality" for your products or services. Although it's simplistic to assert

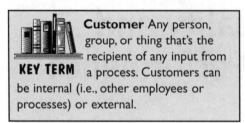

Customer Any person, group, or thing that's the recipient of any input from **KEY TERM** a process. Customers can be internal (i.e., other employees or processes) or external.

"The customer is always right," it's good business to focus on meeting the customer's expectations—and it's "no business at all" after a while if you fail to meet those expectations.

CTQ Characteristics

For every product or service, you need to determine customer expectations, particularly the critical-to-quality (CTQ) characteristics. What do

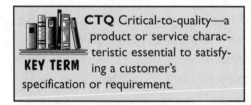

CTQ Critical-to-quality—a product or service characteristic essential to satisfy- **KEY TERM** ing a customer's specification or requirement.

your customers want? What aspects of the product or service are key to your customers? For each aspect, what are your customers' expectations?

For every product or service, there could be dozens or even hundreds of aspects. Focus on those aspects most important to your customers. For every key aspect, there could be several or many expectations.

Identifying CTQ aspects, or factors, is generally a laborious process. In one company, the Six Sigma team analyzed 800–1,000 processes, each of which had 100–120 specifications. The company identified the most critical factors that would lead to greater customer satisfaction, lower costs, and/or greater ease of assembly. The team then prioritized the CTQ factors to be targeted in Six Sigma projects.

I recall a comic strip that showed a professor looking out through his office window at the campus and musing, "This would be a great job—if it weren't for all those students." You may laugh, but many managers and employees seem to feel that way about their customers.

> **HOW DO YOUR CUSTOMERS UNDERSTAND QUALITY?**
> The CTQ concept in Six Sigma allows you to focus on
> improving quality *from the customers' perspective.* Managers
> and employees all have some ideas about what constitutes
> quality for their products or services. That's good, but it doesn't put cash in
> the coffers. Find out which aspects of your products or services are vital to
> the customers and in what ways. Then you can set standards for delivering
> quality that matters to your customers.

Try this simple test: Walk around your company and ask people to complete the following sentence: "Our customers ..." You might be surprised at the perspectives expressed.

You must attract and satisfy and keep customers. Otherwise, you obviously won't stay in business long. But what role do your customers play besides being a source of income?

The better you satisfy your customers (current and potential), the healthier your revenue. You know that. But do you know how to satisfy customers most effectively?

The Voice of the Customer

How do we know what customers need, want, and expect from our products or services? We find out from them. Their input is known in Six Sigma as the Voice of the Customer (VOC). How do we get the VOC?

> **HOW DO YOU LIKE YOUR COFFEE?**
> At a recent conference in a hotel, I asked participants what they
> expected in their coffee breaks. The answer: "Lots of good, hot
> coffee!" When I asked the hotel banquet staff what they
> needed to provide, they agreed on good, hot coffee. But beyond that
> basic agreement, customers and staff differed in their CTQ expectations.
> The staff was concerned with providing linens, china, attractive displays,
> and extra snacks. That may be appropriate for some hotel guests. However,
> these conference participants wanted a fast line for refills, high-capacity
> restrooms nearby, and access to telephones. Of course, customers don't
> want dirty cups or grubby linens, but these customers didn't care much
> about ice sculptures.
> Here's the bottom line. The hotel is putting time and money into things
> that matter less to their customers and missing out on things that their
> customers expect.

Business customers provide requirements and specifications. Sales reps may report on what customers want or don't want, what they need, and what doesn't matter to them. Customers in general may complain, ask questions, give reasons for returning purchases, and offer suggestions for improving products or services. Another way to learn about what customers expect is by staying informed about what competitors are doing with their products or services.

You can also ask your customers and potential customers what they need, what they want, what they like or dislike about your products or services. Companies get the VOC by surveying their customers, asking for feedback on comment forms and their websites, and working with focus groups.

CUSTOMER SATISFACTION

"Customer satisfaction" is an over-worked phrase. But when we break it down using a Six Sigma mindset, we refocus its critical importance.

If you don't understand what your customers want, you can waste time and resources making improvements that don't matter to them—and miss improvements that customers consider vital.

If you want or need to improve products or services, you must identify the factors that your customers consider critical to quality, the CTQs. These are the requirements that are most important to your customers. These CTQs should form definitions of quality for your products or services.

In the case of the airline described in Chapter 1, the customers expected the right luggage would be delivered to the right place at the right time. That simple standard for satisfaction should be the basis for CTQ measurement for customers. Anything less than that is a defect. When the airline fails to meet that most basic expectation, it dissatisfies its customers and is likely to lose some of them—and perhaps others who will hear complaints about lost baggage.

Defects

When you know your customers' CTQs, you can determine what constitutes a defect. What do your customers not want? What makes them less than satisfied with your products or services?

We defined *defect* in Chapter 1 as a "measurable characteristic of the process or its output that is not within the acceptable customer limits, i.e., not conforming to specifications." A defect is any result of your processes that does not meet your customers' expectations. It's a failure to meet a CTQ. You may call it a nonconformity or an error. The terminology doesn't really matter. What matters is that you identify the process results that you need to improve.

Understand Your Processes

When you know what your customers want (the CTQs) and what your customers do *not* want (the defects), you need to know what you are doing to deliver products or services that meet your customers' CTQ expectations. First, you need to identify the processes involved in meeting those CTQ expectations. Then you need to know what's happening in those processes.

It may seem unnecessary to define the word *process*, but it's a word people can understand in various ways. A *process* is a series of activities that convert inputs into outputs. In Six Sigma, a process is initially represented as a unit consisting of five components:

- **Suppliers.** Sources of the inputs into the process.
- **Inputs.** Materials, information, and other resources that are transformed in the process or used in the transformation.
- **Process.** Grouping of activities that transform inputs into outputs.
- **Outputs.** Products or services resulting from the process.
- **Customers.** Recipients of the outputs from the process.

These five components form the SIPOC diagram, a tool that identifies all relevant elements of the process that the project team is responsible for improving.

In the context of identifying a CTQ process, we could specify that it should be a value-added process. Why waste time and effort improving a process that doesn't matter to customers?

> **Process** Series of activities that converts inputs into outputs. In Six Sigma a process consists of five components: suppliers, inputs, process, outputs, and customers.
>
> **KEY TERM**

SIPOC DIAGRAM

TOOLS A SIPOC diagram is a tool used to identify all relevant elements of a process improvement project. It starts simply, as a row of five headings: Suppliers, Inputs, Process, Outputs, Customers. The team builds on it as the project progresses, adding lists and other details.

It should be relatively simple to identify the CTQ processes. What are you doing that matters to your customers? Which processes are involved in aspects of your products or services that your customers consider critical to quality?

The next step requires more work. You map those CTQ processes you've identified. What's happening in those processes?

Then you map the processes related to those CTQs, documenting every step of each CTQ process to determine what information is necessary for targeting improvement areas and fixing problems. We discuss mapping in the chapter on the Define phase.

As you map your processes, pay particular attention to distinguishing between activities that add value to the product or service from the customers' perspective and activities that do not. While the concept of distinguishing between value-added activities and non-value-added activities is simple, it can be difficult to work with that distinction, particularly when the processes have been in place for a while or the employees involved in those activities are secretive, defensive, or territorial.

KEY TERMS **Value-added** Any part of a process for which the customer is willing to pay. Value-added activities would be those involved in producing goods or delivering services.

Non-value-added Any part of a process for which the customer is unwilling to pay. Nonvalue-added activities would include, for example, moving or storing raw products or approvals by various managers before something can happen. Such activities do little or nothing to satisfy customers. They only add costs, so they should be targets for elimination.

Once you've determined the value content of your processes and know which affect CTQ customer issues, you move on to understanding how well your processes are performing.

Determine Your Metrics

How well are you doing what you're doing to meet your customers' CTQ expectations? How can you measure your CTQ processes?

You must be able to measure how your processes are working. If you can measure your processes, you can understand them. If you can understand them, you can correct, control, and improve them. That's the importance of metrics.

The specific metrics depend on the specifics of the processes, of course. We discuss how to establish specific metrics in the chapters on the

> **Metric** Unit of measurement that provides a way to objectively quantify a process. Any measurement **KEY TERM** that helps management understand its operations might be a business metric: number of products completed per hour, percent of defects from a process, hours required to deliver a certain number of outputs or provide a service, and so on.

Define and Measure phases. Now, we limit the discussion of metrics to three that everybody using Six Sigma methodology should know and use.

One of the Six Sigma innovations was to establish universal metrics in terms of opportunities for defects. Six Sigma uses several basic metrics that can be applied to any and every process—DPU, DPO, and DPMO. To calculate the capability of any process, we must be able to use at least these three universal metrics.

DPU, DPO, and DPMO

The first metric is *defects per unit,* or *DPU.* We defined *defect* in Chapter 1 as a measurable characteristic of the process or its output that is not within the acceptable customer limits, i.e., doesn't conform to specifications. For every process, you should define defects for every unit. But what's a unit?

A *unit* is any output of a process that can be measured and evaluated against predetermined criteria or standards. This could be a manufactured gizmo, an assembled widget, a completed form, a product delivered, an interview conducted, and so on. In other words, if it results from a process and you can measure any aspect of it quantitatively, it can be considered a unit.

KEY TERMS

Unit Output of a process that can be measured and evaluated against predetermined criteria or standards.

DPU Defects per unit, calculated as the number of defects divided by the number of units.

DPO Defects per opportunity, calculated as the number of defects divided by the total number of opportunities (i.e., number of units multiplied by number of opportunities for each).

DPU is calculated as the number of defects found divided by the number of units inspected. So you count the gizmos, widgets, forms completed, deliveries, interviews, or whatever results of the process and you count the ways in which those results did not meet customer requirements, specifications, or expectations, then you can calculate the average number of defects.

Another key Six Sigma metric is defects per opportunity, or DPO. We defined *opportunity* in Chapter 1 as any point in a value-added process where a defect could result, where the product or service fails to meet customer requirements, specifications, or expectations.

In determining what should count as an opportunity, be realistic. As one Six Sigma practitioner commented in an online forum, "Some folks think we measure opportunities by counting how many ways something can go wrong. That is a bad approach because it inflates the denominator."

In identifying opportunities for defects, you should involve people who know the process, of course. You should also consider any industry standards for the process and the unit. Assess the relative importance of each type of defect in terms of meeting customer requirements, specifications, or expectations. Finally, you should be practical and allow for the time, effort, and cost of tracking opportunities and defects in process output.

DPO is calculated as the number of defects divided by the total number of opportunities (i.e., number of units multiplied by number of opportunities for each).

Here's a simple example: A truck delivers 100 widgets to a customer across town. You don't count as an opportunity every widget on the truck or every intersection where the trucker could make a wrong turn. Think in terms of opportunities to improve the process. If, in this example, the trucker is delayed because of making a mistake in the directions, a better map or better training in reading maps or maybe a GPS navigator would reduce the chance of similar delays. So the delivery might count as a single opportunity. However, if the 100 widgets go to 100 customers, then there would be 100 opportunities. If the trucker had responsibilities in addition to driving the truck from loading dock to unloading dock, there could be more opportunities.

The next step is easy: Multiply the DPO by 1 million to get the DPMO. As mentioned in Chapter 1, Six Sigma uses the DPMO to represent process performance and capability. Calculating defects in terms of one million opportunities allows for greater precision and convenience. If we identify a large number of opportunities for defects for a particular unit and we detect a small number of defects in that unit, calculating DPO measurements gives us decimals that are difficult to manipulate. For example, instead of playing with numbers like 0.00000047 and 0.000000031, we play with numbers like 0.47 and 0.031.

DPMO enables us to compare different processes. The universal DPMO metric provides a simple quantification of the quality of any process, a simple means by which people in your organization can understand how your processes are performing.

You'll recall from Chapter 1 that sigma levels are based on the number of DPMOs. By calculating quality levels according to the complexity of the product, service, or process, Six Sigma gives you more understand-

---

APPLES AND ORANGES

Here's a simple example. William and Mary both work for Acme Wax Fruit Company. William runs the apple production line, which melts wax cubes, pours the wax into molds, and then dips the resulting item into a wax bath of another color. Mary manages the shipping department for the citrus fruit division. She's responsible for the employees who handle the inventory (oranges, lemons, and limes) in the warehouse, the employees who load the trucks, and the truckers who deliver the goods. The processes that William and Mary manage vary greatly, but since some of the metrics established for them are in terms of DPMO, it's possible to know that they are currently at 81,900 DPMO and 74,700 DPMO, respectively, and set a goal for next year of three sigma—66,800. And that's how, with metrics using DPMO, you can compare apples and oranges!

able and realistic metrics to compare the performance of different prod-ucts, services, or processes.

DPMO is a single numeric value that quantifies how a process is per-forming. Teams can compare DPMO values to identify which processes most need improvement.

The Essential Six Sigma Formula

The DMAIC methodology is a breakthrough strategy. It enables a com-pany to go from a large source of variation to an extremely small one, such as from an 80% yield with a ±5% operating state to a 99% yield with a ±0.25% operating state.

At the heart of Six Sigma is a simple but powerful formula (Figure 2-1). It expresses a fundamental truth: The output of any process (Y) is a function (f) of the inputs (Xs).

$$Y = f(Xs)$$

Figure 2-1. Essential six sigma formula

The Measure and Analyze phases focus on characterizing the process to start understanding the Xs that are driving the Ys. The Improve and Control phases focus on solving the problem of optimizing the process by working on the vital few factors (Xs) that have been statistically identified, reducing the variation, and gaining total control to sustain the gain of the project.

Quality and Metrics, First and Last

This chapter is only an introduction to defining what quality means to your customers and determining how to measure how well your processes are delivering that quality. As mentioned earlier, we discuss establishing specific metrics in the chapters on the Define and Measure phases, where we get into mapping and analyzing processes.

Metrics—both universal (as discussed in this chapter) and specific to your processes—are essential to using Six Sigma. For Six Sigma to work optimally, the extraordinary commitment of resources throughout your organization must be validated continuously. The best way to validate the investment is through data. You need metrics to quantify what you can expect from your people and processes and to quantify the progress you're making toward the goals based on those expectations.

Manager's Checklist for Chapter 2

☑ Define quality from your customers' perspective. Six Sigma requires that you know what your customers want, not what you *think* they want. What are their CTQ criteria?

☑ Understand your processes. Map all the steps, paying particular attention to distinguishing between activities that do and do not add value to the product or service from the customers' perspective.

☑ Identify every possible defect in each product or service that you're targeting with Six Sigma.

☑ Identify every possible opportunity for defects to occur. You need this information to know how to calculate DPMO and sigma level—and to begin working on process defects.

☑ Metrics—both universal and specific to your processes—are essential to using Six Sigma. You need metrics to quantify what you can expect and to quantify your progress.

The Right Way to Implement Six Sigma

The difference between failure and success is doing a thing *nearly* right and doing it *exactly* right."
—Edward Simmons (1852–1931)

O ver the years since 1994, back when the first large-scale deployment of Six Sigma took place, things have changed significantly. The world economy is totally different. The Six Sigma implementation plan (aka deployment model) has evolved to a new level. Companies are not as much interested in large-scale, massive training programs, which is good, since this was never the right model for Six Sigma.

Six Sigma: The Early Years and Implementation Flaws

When my company started the Six Sigma deployment at AlliedSignal (later acquired by Honeywell) in 1993 and, more important, at GE in 1996, Six Sigma deployment was flawed from the onset. We started waves of training—aptly named for the tsunami effect they had on the organization infrastructure. We typically started with the best-of-the-best employees, the company's high-potential employees. (That is one of two things that have remained constant among the critical factors of the implementation plan. The other is project selection, which is discussed in Chapter 4 on the Define phase.) Imagine the reality of this plan. We take around 50–75 of the company's top people and send them to one week of Six Sigma training every month over a four-month period—and then their jobs no longer exist because they are reassigned full-time to becoming "black belts." They're working on chronic and serious problems in projects that will result in reducing defects and making a major improvement in the bottom line. So we now have 50–75 people showing up for class on Monday morning, in cohorts of 25 one week apart, to learn the Six Sigma method so they can apply it to the project assigned to them.

The first flaw in the large-scale implementation that should be obvious is that these people were doing important work, which has now been totally disrupted and, in most cases, still must be done by someone. So you have an immediate gap in human resources, and requests for replacements to fill those gaps are usually denied by the powers that be. Not a good way to engage management support.

Now you believe that you have full-time resources, but what really happened in most cases was that the full-time resource was actually only a part-time resource transitioning into the role of a full-time black belt, a transition that resulted in a major delay in implementing Six Sigma and getting results.

The reality of the Six Sigma initiative at General Electric that has never been publicly known is that for the first six months it was "an up-at-dawn, pride-swallowing siege," as Jerry Maguire said of his job in the movie of that name. Management and leadership could not admit to the flaw, because significant finances had already been invested in the initiative, so we worked our way through it like giving birth to a new method.

There were 50–75 people asking for data, measurements, and other resources in the organization to become team members to support the new Six Sigma effort. The same person measuring one project was in some cases also a resource in demand by 10 black belts requiring support. GE would never admit defeat in a large-scale deployment as that's against its religion. Fortunately, it had plenty of resources to correct, rework, delay, and adjust to ensure success.

Don't get me wrong here: GE achieved the same level of results, but the climb involved months of delays and false starts and if it weren't for the sustained pure energy of Jack Welch ... well, they made it happen!

Not every company has such deep resources or the outstanding leadership of a Jack Welch. For our purposes here, we need a more economically realistic approach that yields a long-term genetically embedded culture change.

A More Realistic Approach to Six Sigma

Until now I've never written about this new, proven implementation strategy. It enables companies implementing Six Sigma to avoid the flaws in the conventional deployment model, specifically, the widespread changes and financial problems that seem inevitable in immediate large-scale implementation.

Step 1: Try and Demonstrate

It's simple, really: You start small, with a tryout of Six Sigma on a tough problem, to demonstrate Six Sigma and the impressive results it can achieve. It's what I call a "try-and-demonstrate" approach.

I use as an example one of my recent clients, Gates Corporation. Gates is a single-digit billion-dollar, privately held industrial engineering and manufacturing company based in Denver, with more than 14,500 employees in manufacturing and sales operations in North and South America, Europe, Asia, Australia, and the Middle East. The president and COO, Al Powers, was one of my CEO clients years ago.

I called Al a few years ago to catch up with him. In the course of our conversation, Al asked if I could come to Iola, Kansas to work on a chronic issue in the Gates Corporation hose plant there.

He explained that a consultant had been helping implement Six Sigma at the plant, but the projects weren't generating the results expected. Al wondered whether the Six Sigma methodology was being properly implemented. He wanted me to take a try-and-demonstrate approach.

I agreed to come and use Six Sigma to work on a defect that had plagued rubber hose manufacturers for 40 years. We found a solution to the problem in about four months, and it took an additional four months to work out the resources and control plans needed to sustain the gain. The solution resulted in major residual benefits across the entire production line of that type of hose.

I won't go into detail about the defect, but the solution and the root causes of the problem had never been identified in any way for 40 years. We demonstrated that Six Sigma actually works: It solved a real problem, resulting in eliminating a defect, reducing costs, and giving the company a competitive edge. This success got the attention of leadership and middle management and may have inspired them to go to the next level.

The key point here is that demonstrating the power of Six Sigma gives people reason to believe. Even some of the naysayers actually gained a keen interest in Six Sigma. This demonstration started to create a *pull* system, as opposed to a *push* system. In other words, people in the organization were requesting (pulling) Six Sigma techniques and resources, in contrast with the usual situation in which the powers that be force (push) Six Sigma on them.

To ensure a pull system for Six Sigma, the project you select for the demonstration must aim to resolve an old problem of mythic proportions, a defect long considered impossible to fix—such a challenge that when you announce you want to find a solution, you get a combination of laughter

---

SMART

MANAGING

SHOW, DON'T JUST TELL

In 1997 I was flying to the UK with one of my colleagues, Richard Schroeder (coauthor of *Six Sigma: The Breakthrough Management Strategy Revolutionizing the World's Top Corporations*), to work with a new client. Richard is a CEO, a marketing and sales type of executive not so much into the working details of Six Sigma. Out of the blue, I started talking about how the power of the Six Sigma method is that it can truly get to the root of the problem.

He looked me square in the eyes and said, "Greg, do you really know what we are selling to these corporate leaders?"

"What?"

"We're selling hope."

"So," I asked, "they must have faith?" I told him that it sounded more like a religion than a methodology for fixing problems. "That's *not* what I sell."

Companies these days never invest in hope. We must demonstrate real solutions. That's how you get a little buy-in and start the pull system required to build momentum for the Six Sigma implementation.

and comments such as "Good luck with that!" and "Hell will freeze over before you fix that problem." You get my point. That's the first step.

Step 2: Align the Leaders

The second step is to align the organization's leadership to ensure they will continue the Six Sigma journey. (It's definitely not a destination.) You do this to build the method part of your culture—your way of doing business, your language—built into the organization's genetic code (to borrow the words of Jack Welch when he proclaimed that Six Sigma was the most important initiative the company had undertaken—"part of the genetic code of our future leadership").

Leadership alignment means that the organization's leaders actively and visibly support the program, which makes the difference between real success and halfway to failure. It's critical to the program's success, a fundamental requirement. If you lack leadership alignment, I suggest that you do a one-off demonstration for results purposes and do *not* go to the next step.

One measure of successful leadership alignment is the velocity of project completions, a direct indication of leadership support. Basically, if your implementation is a success, the rate of project completion is between four and six projects per year for each certified black belt. Here's a simple example of failure: You certified 15 black belts on April 14, 2014 and as of April 15, 2015 the number of projects completed is 20, when it should be at least 60, so you do *not* have the support and alignment to sustain any more black belts or even justify keeping your current black belts. You don't do Six Sigma halfway.

Step 3: Get the Best Black Belt Candidates

The third step is to screen and select your best-of-the-best people to participate in the Six Sigma journey. We did a study of hundreds of black belts who were trained and practicing during the mid-1990s. We reviewed the results obtained by each of those black belts in terms of the financial outcomes of their projects and their ability to complete tasks for project successes. In addition, we reviewed failed black belt candidates and successful black belts. The outcome of the study was a selection tool, which is presented later in this chapter, with a list of 11 criteria and a rating scale for ensuring maximum probability of success. I strongly encourage you to use this tool, which has been proven to work for more than 50 deployment clients.

Step 4: Choose Projects with High Financial Impact

The next step is to select projects to solve problems that will have a high financial impact. (Project selection is covered in Chapter 4.) Let's assume you have a list of problems in your business and a list of your specific business functions and, by the way, you also know the financial impact that each project could make. Now, match your highest-impact projects with your high-potential black belt candidates.

The Crucial Difference

Here I want to deviate from the large-scale GE implementation model.

The first list of projects consists of only 8–10 projects, with a strategy to continue building on that list immediately. The first list of black belt candidates consists of only 8–10 individuals. Why? We're implementing Six Sigma in a highly surgical manner—not a shotgun blast of resources at a lot of targets, but a focused shot at specific, high-priority targets. The immediate goal is to generate momentum for change and to accumulate project wins to demonstrate the power of Six Sigma and build the pull system. Our goal is to ensure a 100% success rate with all black belt candidates.

We're also automatically screening the higher-potential candidates for higher training, to transform them into master black belts. Use internal screening methods to find the top performers among the pool of high-potential black belt candidates. Typically two or three top performers will go into master black belt training.

This is part of the process of transitioning the Six Sigma consultant out of the organization and achieving Six Sigma self-sufficiency. Your master black belts start to take over high-level projects, screen new black belt and green belt projects, and train belt candidates. You now are growing an internal base of Six Sigma resources to sustain your Six Sigma program.

Big Benefits of a More Realistic Approach

Getting through the four steps takes two to three years. It's a self-funding and self-sustaining system, as your master black belts, black belts, and green belts are typically saving between $500,000 and $1.5 million of growth profit per year. The typical ROI for a single black belt is between 500 and 800 percent. Remember: The cost of the program is paid through the savings generated by the try-and-demonstrate project.

This new implementation model avoids the high cost of replacing high-potential candidates, avoids the high demand on resources (notably use of data systems and time spent in Six Sigma project activities), and reduces leadership distractions in general. Starting small and building capability over time generates momentum and creates a sustained pull system.

Currently in the Gates Corporation we are through the first year. People—both managers and employees—in locations around the world are requesting to be trained, and plant managers are asking when their plants can be involved and how they can get started. Gates has 18 solid, successful wins that are in the Control phase—two projects by each of nine black belts in the first year. To become certified, a black belt candidate must complete two projects during the training year. Why? Because the first project success could be a fluke and because it's a test for the business to sustain the gain of the Six Sigma implementation.

You can control the rollout and ensure the focused support and success along with tracking future projects at the black belt level. More is typically better, but not so much in the Six Sigma "big bang theory." A small, focused pull system is the optimal implementation plan. As long as you follow the basic principles expressed in the following list, you can ensure that your efforts will work most efficiently and effectively for lasting results.

Readying the Organization

So now you know what to do and what not to do. It's time to figure out how to prepare your organization for the Six Sigma journey. It's important and necessary for employees at every level to understand and embrace the initiative.

Assess Your Readiness for Six Sigma

As I've repeated throughout these first few chapters, you must have data for Six Sigma to succeed. Do you have any basic measurements in place for your various business functions? Does your organization collect reliable data in a structured manner?

Whatever you're doing or planning to do, it's important that your information be accurate and credible. You must also be able to define success for every step in every process, so you can determine what constitutes a defect or an error. And you need to know how to assess your Six Sigma readiness. You can use the following checklist to do that.

SIX SIGMA READINESS CHECKLIST

If you agree with the following statements and can answer the questions, you may already be on the Six Sigma journey.

1. Customers have critical-to-quality expectations.
   Can you list your customers' top four expectations?
   1. _____
   2. _____
   3. _____
   4. _____

2. We are in business to achieve a phenomenal customer satisfaction rate that exceeds critical-to-quality expectations.
   Can you quantify your customers' current level of satisfaction?
   Yes _____ No _____
   If yes, what is it, on a scale of 1–10? _____
   How has it changed over the last five years?

   _____

3. We strive to produce profitable bottom-line results. We are in business to profitably serve customers!
   List your company's profits for the last five years:
   Year 1 $_____
   Year 2 $_____
   Year 3 $_____
   Year 4 $_____
   Year 5 $_____

4. We have repetitive processes in our business that create products and services for our customers.
   List four major repetitive processes in your business:
   Process #1_____
   Process #2_____
   Process #3_____
   Process #4_____

How many times do you do these processes per year?

Process #1 _____

Process #2 _____

Process #3 _____

Process #4 _____

5. In our processes, the goal is to create knowledge and take action to reduce cycle time, defects, and variations. For Processes #1 and #2 above, give the cycle time and the rate of defects or yield.

	Cycle Time	% Defects or Yield
Process #1 Baseline:	_____	_____
Process #2 Baseline:	_____	_____

6. We create knowledge about our processes by collecting data and stating the problem in statistical terms, such as the mean and standard deviation of the process.

   Does your company know the vital statistics of Processes #1–4 listed above?   Yes _____ No _____

7. We share our knowledge to ensure that everyone understands and benefits from that knowledge.

   How does your company transfer knowledge?

   _____

   What velocity is involved in that knowledge transfer?

   _____

   Is there an infrastructure (e.g., intranet or database sharing) in place?

   _____

8. We as a company achieve our goals, which result in sustained and satisfied internal and external customers.

   What are two goals that have been met in the last two years?

   Goal #1_____

   Goal #2 _____

Were you able to understand and answer every question? If so, congratulations! If not, then your company is an excellent candidate for doing Six Sigma!

Key Players

We've mentioned the key players and some aspects of their roles. Basically, there are five key players whose roles are listed below:

- **Executive Leaders and Champions.** To commit to Six Sigma and promote it throughout the organization
- **Champion.** To fight for the cause of black belts and remove barriers
- **Master Black Belt.** To serve as trainer, mentor, and guide
- **Black Belts.** To work full-time on projects
- **Green Belts.** To assist black belts part-time

> **SMART**
>
> **MANAGING**
>
> **WITH ROLES MUST COME RESPONSIBILITY**
>
> Each participant in the Six Sigma initiative, regardless of his or her role, must have full responsibility for a specific area. Simply put, to be responsible is to be accountable, trustworthy, and dependable. It's important that all participants recognize this as their personal charter: From green belt to executive, they need to exercise responsibility in all they do to achieve optimum outcomes.

It's vital to understand and define key roles from the start. All key players should know what's expected of them and how the roles work together in the Six Sigma initiative. Each of the roles has clearly defined responsibilities.

Executive Leaders and Champions

The key role of executive leaders is to decide to do Six Sigma and, as we've mentioned, to publicly endorse it throughout the organization. Company leaders must kick off and reinforce the comprehensive scope of Six Sigma to engage everyone's support and participation. It's important for Six Sigma to be a company-wide initiative; that point cannot be emphasized enough. And as you begin this business-changing enterprise, visible leadership is crucial. It rallies the employees, it lends legitimacy to your projects, and it sends the clearest signal that Six Sigma and your targeted outcomes are major company priorities.

But what do the responsibilities of executive leaders entail? A few essential aspects help build and round out the foundation for successful executive leadership responsibility. The executive champion is an evolved role in the Six Sigma world. This role is a side-by-side: The executive is focused only on Six Sigma outcomes and has just as much executive power as the president. The executive champion is in charge of the Six Sigma program.

Here's a real-world example. John is the executive champion for one of my recent clients. He reports directly to the president; however, the president has given him parallel authority and responsibility to focus on Six Sigma outcomes. He is sure there are no barriers in resources, including capital requirements if necessary, and that additional resources are available. He approved of the Six Sigma projects in parallel with me, created a bimonthly progress update, and ensured that accountability for project local champions (to be covered next) was in place for tracking progress. He has led by example, by learning the Six Sigma language and methodology and he has ensured that any local leader who was not aligned was out—"Fix it or get out!"

His job is the relentless pursuit for perfection and immediate results using the Six Sigma methodology. This client had 100% success—not 99% or 80%—in all projects with a major financial result.

John, the executive champion, showed *determination to get results*. He was resolute in believing that Six Sigma would succeed. After the initial fanfare of introducing Six Sigma, the executive champion determines how to get the training, understand the savings, enforce the use of metrics, showcase black belt achievements, mark key milestones, and keep the initiative on track.

Jack Welch, the CEO who started Six Sigma at GE, called it "part of the genetic code" of future leadership at that company. Welch could be considered the ideal executive leader for Six Sigma because an executive's responsibility, ultimately, is to make sure that Six Sigma becomes part of the company's "genetic code." From the top down and throughout all points in the organization, executive leaders can inspire and promote a Six Sigma culture that continually produces results.

John, the executive champion, actively displayed confidence—not only in the Six Sigma methodology, but also in the people charged with making it work. By actively backing up their confidence with rewards and incentives, company leaders inspire sustained commitment and effort on the part of employees. When an executive shows employees that he or she believes in them, supports their success, and applauds their talents, employees respond in kind. Confidence is a powerful motivator.

Bear in mind that confidence isn't all compliments and congratulations. It can be supported by the facts and figures that emerge from project metrics. Executives can point to specific outcomes as proof that confidence in a given champion, black belt, or project team has been validated. As Dizzy Dean, professional baseball player in the 30s and 40s, put it so eloquently, "It ain't braggin' if you can back it up."

Finally, the executive champion supports it all with integrity. John always stated what he would do and then followed up with actions. Basically, executive champions *need to do what they say they're going to do*. This inspires ever-increasing confidence among project team members that an executive's word is good and there's substance behind the statements. By following through on commitments and staying true to a stated purpose, executives demonstrate a high standard of ethical leadership. Integrity stimulates loyalty and respect, both of which motivate employees across the organization.

Champions

Champions are critical to the success or failure of any Six Sigma project. The word champion goes back to Latin (*campus*). In the Middle Ages a champion was someone who took the field to battle for a cause. In Six Sigma, a champion is an advocate who fights for the cause of black belts and removes barriers—functional, financial, personal, etc.—so that black belts can do their work.

Champions are closest to the process, and it's no exaggeration to say that they "own" it in every respect. Depending on the company's size, champions are drawn from the ranks of the executives and managers. Champions are responsible for the daily oversight and management of each critical element. They report to senior management about project progress and they support their teams. Champions must be sure that the projects they select align with the executive strategy and that the projects can be readily understood and embraced by project teams.

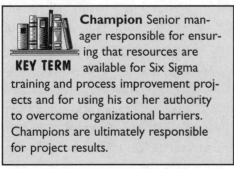

Champion Senior manager responsible for ensuring that resources are **KEY TERM** available for Six Sigma training and process improvement projects and for using his or her authority to overcome organizational barriers. Champions are ultimately responsible for project results.

Champions select black belt candidates, identify project areas, and establish clear and measurable project goals. They do whatever it takes to keep the projects on schedule.

> ## WHAT MAKES A GOOD CHAMPION?
>
> At a manufacturing company implementing Six Sigma, a desig-
> nated champion regularly met with his black belts. At one
> report-out meeting, a black belt informed him that she needed
> to purchase and install a table for sorting defects off-line. It would cost
> about $17,000, but it would provide an alternative to shutting down the
> entire line, which would cost far more. The controller told her to go
> through the normal requisition process, and she'd have her table in about
> four months. That delay would have killed the project right then and there:
> To allow the project to be subject to "business as usual" would have shown
> little real commitment to supporting Six Sigma. So the champion asked for
> the data to support her request, analyzed it, agreed with it, and got immedi-
> ate executive sign-off on securing a table the following week.
>
> This is the stuff of a good champion: removing barriers and showing that
> she or he and upper management are aligned with and committed to Six
> Sigma. The champion does whatever it takes to support the black belts.

Champions must be fully engaged in the process, allotting at least 20–30 percent of their time to ensuring that black belts are making progress on their projects. They must identify and remove obstacles so the black belts can focus on the project and achieve the bottom-line outcomes. You can't do that from the sidelines; champions must be in the thick of the battle!

The champion selects the project and monitors project team performance. The champion acts as advocate and defender, as mentor and coach. He or she is ultimately responsible for the Six Sigma project. A champion must thoroughly understand the strategy and discipline of Six Sigma and be able to educate others about its tools and implementation. A champion directs and mobilizes the teams to make lasting changes. She or he also ensures that the teams share what they learn; they transfer the knowledge into other areas and increase the results exponentially.

Master Black Belts

In reading this book, you're taking an important first step as a Six Sigma champion. This role is often initially executed by a member of your implementation partner's team. The master black belt serves as trainer, mentor, and guide. He or she teaches you the ropes, helps you select the right people, and assists in selecting projects.

KEY TERMS

Implementation partner Outside expert who introduces Six Sigma, trains employees, and supports the initiative.

Master black belt Six Sigma expert responsible for implementing the Six Sigma methodology within an organization. Master black belts train and mentor black belts and green belts, help select and charter process improvement projects, ensure the integrity of project activities and the use of Six Sigma methodology and tools, and serve as resources, particularly in the use of statistical tools. Master black belts have more extensive and intensive training than black belts. They also have experience in leading process improvement projects and in training and mentoring black belts and green belts.

The master black belt is an expert in Six Sigma tools and tactics and is a valuable resource in terms of technical and historical expertise. Teacher, mentor, and lead change agent, the master black belt ensures that the necessary infrastructure is in place and that black belts are trained. He or she focuses 100 percent on process improvement.

A key aspect of the role is the capacity to skillfully facilitate problem-solving without actually taking over a project. In this way, you and your team have the security of knowing that you've chosen the best project, that you're using the tools correctly, and that you will succeed—all without losing autonomy or giving up responsibility.

A master black belt is an invaluable asset as you begin your Six Sigma initiative—coordinating and collaborating with you and upper management, advising and coaching black belts, and keeping the champion focused on what's important in selecting projects and implementing Six Sigma.

Once your Six Sigma initiative is well under way, once you've established all the necessary elements, designated and trained people in their roles, started projects, and garnered some results, you can graduate some of your black belts to assume the role of master black belt. As your black belts gain experience and some become master black belts, you're on your way to sustaining the success of your Six Sigma initiative.

Black Belts

Black belts work full-time on selected projects. As team leaders and project heads, black belts are central to Six Sigma success. They are trained to dig into the chronic and high-impact issues and fix them using Six

Sigma techniques and practices. It sounds simple; they fix the problems, get rid of the defects, and find the money.

> **Black belt** Full-time Six Sigma team leader responsible for implementing process improvement projects under the direction of a champion. Black belts are trained in the use of the Six Sigma methodology and tools and have experience in completing process improvement projects. **KEY TERM**

The black belt role is one of great responsibility and discipline. Black belts work their projects full time, 100 percent dedicated to fixing problems and making sure that what gets improved *stays* improved!

Selecting Black Belts

As we've discussed, black belt projects are central to Six Sigma, with important responsibilities as technical experts, team leaders, and project heads. A champion must take great care in designating employees to become black belts. So, how does a champion select black belt candidates?

Not every employee is black belt material. It's a full-time discipline that combines leadership ability, technical skills, some statistical knowledge, the ability to communicate clearly, and motivated curiosity. The sidebar

---

RATING A BLACK BELT CANDIDATE

Here's a quick way to evaluate a potential black belt. Rate the employee in each of these 11 key areas, on a scale of 1–5 (1 = unacceptable, 2 = below average, 3 = average, 4 = above average, 5 = excellent).

Process and product knowledge _____
Basic statistical knowledge _____
Knowledge about your organization _____
Communication skills _____
Self-starter, motivated _____
Open-minded _____
Eager to learn about new ideas _____
Desire to drive change _____
Team player _____
Respected _____
Results track record _____
Total: _____

A candidate who scores at least 38 has excellent black belt potential. A candidate who scores 35 should become a green belt.

"Rating a Black Belt Candidate" provides an organized approach to evaluating black belt potential.

Green Belts

Green belts assist black belts in their functional area. They work on projects part-time, usually in a specific, limited area, on projects within their regular jobs. They share with black belts their knowledge of the processes and their outputs, whether products or services.

KEY TERM **Green belt** Employee who participates in Six Sigma process improvement projects as part of his or her job and may be responsible for leading a process improvement team in smaller projects, with a black belt as mentor. Green belts are trained in the use of the Six Sigma methodology and tools and have extensive knowledge of processes and products or services.

Green belts also help black belts accomplish more in less time. They may help collect or analyze data, run experiments, or perform other important project tasks. They are team members with enough understanding of Six Sigma to share the tools with other employees and transform company culture from the ground up. Working in a complementary fashion with the executive leaders, champions, and black belts, green belts are essential "worker bees," driving bottom-line results.

Communicate!

Communication is key. Again, the clearest way to show the importance of Six Sigma and your investment in it is to communicate with the Six Sigma players throughout the implementation. Tell the story as often as you can.

TRICKS OF THE TRADE

INTRODUCING THE SIX SIGMA INITIATIVE
An effective way to kick off Six Sigma is a letter of introduction from the CEO or president, distributed to every employee, to communicate the importance of Six Sigma and express executive commitment to its success. Adapt the sample letter on the next page to your situation.

Use all the tools available, such as your company intranet, newsletter, or other communication channels. Post information on what, how, and when you plan to kick off your Six Sigma projects. Publicize the roles and responsibilities of every person participating in the Six Sigma process. State clearly the purpose of your projects: Outline the outcomes expected and communicate how the entire company benefits from your efforts.

As discussed earlier, it's crucial to have the full support of senior management and to make it known. You can communicate this through vehicles such as e-mail and corporate newsletters, but you should also find a way for your company leaders to directly address employees. Use videos and company meetings to get the message out—your executives are indispensable to getting company-wide buy-in. With the consistent and continual reinforcement of their support, you can reduce fear of change and inform employees about how they are all part of the success or failure of what you're doing. Here is a sample letter of introduction for a Six Sigma initiative.

From: [President, CEO, or other executive]
To: All Employees
Subject: Six Sigma Success

The world in which we're competing here at [company name] keeps changing. Competition is stronger than ever. Customers have more choices and demand higher quality and faster delivery. Profit margins are shrinking across our industry. To compete effectively in this environment and deliver on our commitments to ourselves, our customers, and our shareholders, we need a strategy to improve our performance.

That strategy is Six Sigma. Six Sigma is the best way for us to improve our performance, our processes, and our products and services.

The term *sigma* is a measurement that will tell us how well we are doing in our efforts to reduce waste and defects in our processes so we can provide better products and services and reduce our costs. Six Sigma is a methodology that will help us do that.

You will all have the chance to get acquainted with the Six Sigma methodology and receive essential training. In addition, some of you will receive further training so you can use the Six Sigma methods and tools to improve our processes.

Six Sigma requires all of us at all levels to think differently about our processes and to work differently. I urge you to support our Six Sigma initiative to provide higher-quality products and services and reduce costs. As we reach our goals, you will be recognized and rewarded for your dedication to the success of this initiative.

Our executive staff is committed to the program, and we have already received training in the Six Sigma methodology. We will be training participants at all levels. On [date] we will begin training those employees who

> will lead our process improvement teams as project leaders (known as *black belts* in the Six Sigma terminology). We have selected [consultant company name] to help us begin using Six Sigma to improve our processes so that we may all benefit.
>
> Again, your support and your participation are vital to our success in this initiative. Together, we can improve how we are working here and achieve better results from our efforts. Please join me in commiting to this exciting initiative.

Train!

After the head of the company has introduced the Six Sigma initiative to all employees, the initiative is presented to executives and managers in special sessions to reinforce their understanding and support. Beyond that, executive training should be offered to all senior managers, and champion training should be offered to managers at all levels.

Executive training should include an overview of Six Sigma, a review of case studies, related product and service demonstrations, deployment strategies, and an introduction to the scientific tools and methods, statistical analysis, improvements, measurements, and management controls.

Champion training should provide the managerial and technical knowledge necessary to plan and implement Six Sigma projects and mentor black belts. The goal is to transfer and reinforce fundamental Six Sigma strategies, tactics, and tools. Training should cover the principles, tools, and applications of Six Sigma, including deployment tactics and strategies for establishing metrics, selecting black belts and projects, and implementing Six Sigma.

After introducing Six Sigma to executives and managers and determining who will receive executive and champion training, the next steps in preparing for the initiative are to order training materials, select black belt candidates, and schedule training.

Infrastructure

As you compile your list of black belt candidates, you develop job descriptions for their new roles and coordinate with your human resources department to post them. Human resources should also benchmark compensation plans that reward black belts and their teams upon project completions.

Once you've selected your black belt candidates, determined how they will be rewarded, and decided what your projects will entail, it's time to start the training. This involves coordinating all training site logistics, ensuring that you and your executive team are ready to serve as champions, and ensuring that the training materials and instructors are ready to go. Then you communicate with the black belt candidates about the training schedule and prep them for their first day of class.

Critical to the success of your black belts is the on-site support of an experienced master black belt, usually provided by the outside consultant. A master black belt guides and coaches the black belt candidates and works with the champions to overcome obstacles. A master black belt also builds relationships with company leaders and informs and educates them on the progress of their Six Sigma initiative.

There are also periodic, formal meetings involving champions, senior leaders, and the outside consultant to discuss the progress of the Six Sigma initiative. The review's primary purpose is to ensure that the project teams are meeting their objectives and the initiative is staying on track.

What to Expect from Outside Consultants

In this chapter, I've talked about outside consultants. Since I am one of these, you may be thinking, "OK, here comes the sales pitch." Well, no, just a few words about why you should select an outside consultant to help you start your Six Sigma initiative and how to choose appropriately.

First, you need to work with someone who preaches *and* practices Six Sigma. When you're talking about implementing a strategy that's going to change not only your outcomes, but also your processes and deployment of your people, you'd better get it right the first time. You need to choose an outside consultant/partner with a demonstrated track record of being a real "money miner" for client companies. After all, you want your investment to pay off as quickly and effectively as possible. Your consultant should help you lay the groundwork and erect the required infrastructure so you can move quickly toward self-sufficiency.

The consultant should focus on knowledge transfer, showing you how to solve problems through the most effective methods and fix

ARE THEY IN THE SAME BOAT?
A quick way to distinguish among outside consultants is to look at how they structure their own employee reward systems. We all need to make money, of course. But here's a big difference. Some consultants are rewarded for *time*, based on their billable hours. Others are rewarded for *results*, based on the speed and size of the client's ROI. Both groups of consultants are committed to your success in theory, but only consultants in the latter category are in the same boat as you, rowing toward the same objective—financial results.

process defects with the right tools so you can transfer that knowledge throughout your organization.

Finally, when choosing a Six Sigma consultant, check credentials. There are many consultants out there purporting to be Six Sigma experts, so you need to sort out fiction from fact. Ask for proof of their claims: Request references and actual case studies from bona fide clients. You don't want anecdotal discussion; you want to see the actual link to the clients' outcomes. You want proof of results—after all, that's what Six Sigma is all about.

Getting Started: The Dos

DO focus on results. Have a clear vision of where you are and where you want to be in terms of decreasing costs and increasing bottom-line profits. Keep track of the projects with a simple spreadsheet. There are a lot of project-tracking systems available. You don't need cool software with whiz-bang GUI tools. The goal is to focus on project results.

DO embrace customers. Remember your customers' critical-to-quality (CTQ) expectations? Achieving phenomenal business growth depends on how well you understand and meet those expectations. So stay in touch with customers and keep current on what they want from you in terms of price, quality, and delivery. Remember: It's not about what *you think* they want, but what *they say* they want.

DO plan for success. Proper planning will help you meet your goals. Planning provides the milestones and progress reports that indicate how well and how fast you're moving toward your goals.

DO communicate the commitment throughout the company. Tell everyone what you're doing and what you intend to accomplish. From the CEO to production line employees, every member of the organization should have a vested interest and role in your Six Sigma projects—a sense of ownership goes a long way toward driving true commitment and enthusiasm at every level.

DO demonstrate the commitment of company leaders. Make sure your company leaders actively show their own commitment to your Six Sigma success. They need to show all employees that they're prepared to do whatever it takes to get the results you want. They do this by serving as mentors and champions, freeing up company resources and breaking down barriers to support your projects.

DO empower your key human resources. Pick the right people to lead your Six Sigma project teams—and empower those key players. Throughout the Six Sigma phases of Define, Measure, Analyze, Improve, and Control, make sure that your black belts and team members have the essential quality tools for every project.

DO provide on-site mentoring for black belts. As part of that empowerment, you must assure your black belts of your total support for their projects. Their access to information or data, from within and from outside of your company, and their interpretation of it must be unrestricted. By applying Six Sigma statistical tools in tandem with critical data, black belts can mine hidden dollars. As long as you and other champions and your implementation partner are available on-site to mentor them, black belts will provide the ROI you want.

DO choose an implementation partner who will actively assist in screening and selecting Six Sigma projects. A qualified outside expert can provide substantial value in helping you select not only the right project, but the right people to run it.

DO be patient at the inception of your Six Sigma initiative. Six Sigma projects require the front-end commitment of training, time, and resources to deliver results. You and your employees have to learn how to select projects, develop metrics, and assign key roles. All that takes time. Proper planning makes for profitable outcomes—you can't rush results.

DO claim and advertise early wins. Although you need to be patient as your projects get under way, it's important to communicate and celebrate each milestone of success. This keeps your team's enthusiasm high and demonstrates how Six Sigma works. Tell employees, upper management, customers, and vendors—they need to know the value of your efforts every step of the way.

DO benchmark. Benchmarking is a key step. By formulating a benchmark plan that looks at both internal and external performance standards, you can conduct the right gap analysis to know where you are and where you should be.

DO establish project baselines and goals. You need to know your current defect levels, your defect-reduction targets, and how much you want to save. Then you'll have the right baselines and goals to measure the progress of your projects.

DO get advance buy-in from your controller. It's important—especially when you're talking about company money—to be in sync with the company controller! You need to operate from the same monetary baseline: You need to agree on how you calculate real savings and how you distinguish between hard dollars and soft dollars. If you work together, the controller can verify your results, which further validates your Six Sigma work.

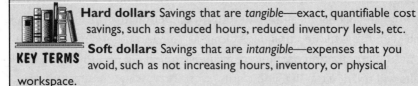

KEY TERMS   **Hard dollars** Savings that are *tangible*—exact, quantifiable cost savings, such as reduced hours, reduced inventory levels, etc.
Soft dollars Savings that are *intangible*—expenses that you avoid, such as not increasing hours, inventory, or physical workspace.

Getting Started: The Don'ts

DON'T make Six Sigma a massive "training" exercise. Six Sigma focuses on real, tangible financial results. You and your staff need to learn how to implement it and get started. You don't need to send your employees to seminar after seminar to further develop their Six Sigma skills. Of course, they need to know what they're doing, but once they're trained as black belts, they'll know exactly what they need to do and can use what they've learned. This is all about getting results in bottom-line profitability.

DON'T take a "big bang" approach to Six Sigma. Don't train all employees at once to be Six Sigma practitioners. Starting with the right people and the right projects is far more effective. Most organizations can't manage a lot of changes simultaneously or support large numbers of black belts or projects. Start small and focus on capturing clear gains project by project. As you achieve results, other company divisions can embrace the methodology.

DON'T focus resources on reworking training material. A big part of implementing Six Sigma is training. While you certainly want to train your people well, particularly your black belts, you don't want to spend excessive time tweaking training materials to fit your exact business model. You should certainly relate training materials to your business focus, but recognize the overall and adaptable nature of Six Sigma and get busy applying it, not discussing it.

DON'T let the controller waffle about your savings calculations. Controllers play an important role and must be included in your Six Sigma initiative at the outset. They need to know that your executive leadership expects them to cooperate and support your efforts. Controllers who refuse to acknowledge soft vs. hard dollar savings can really hurt a Six Sigma project. Make sure you and the controller are in agreement on how you define and assign savings to your projects.

DON'T skip steps. It may be tempting to speed up a project by skipping necessary steps in Six Sigma, but then you won't get the information you need to solve the problem in question. Let the data tell the story. You need to dwell in the realm of quantifiable facts and not in assumptions. You apply statistical measurements and metrics to analyze the issues to make your case with data—not by opinion—as to why and how you can make lasting changes.

Executive Overview of DMAIC

The upcoming Chapters 4–8 present the five phases of the Six Sigma methodology—Define, Measure, Analyze, Improve, and Control (DMAIC). Here is a brief introduction to these phases:

- **Define.** The Define phase determines the project's purpose, objec-

SMART

MANAGING

SHOW ME THE MONEY!

Sometimes controllers can be Six Sigma barriers, as they fear their budgets will be cut if they report the money saved by your projects. For instance, in some companies, if a project saves $10 million in a $100 million budget, the savings will be eliminated, forcing controllers to operate with a $90 million budget. You and your executive champion need to communicate that the purpose of your Six Sigma projects is to *save* "hidden" money, not to *eliminate* it. Although you want to drive that hidden revenue to the bottom line, you will also use it in other areas. This way, Six Sigma projects work to *reduce costs*, not to *slash budgets*. When the controller understands that, she or he will probably want the projects to succeed as much as you do.

tives, and scope; collects information on the customers and the process involved; and specifies the project deliverables to customers (internal and external).

- **Measure.** In the Measure phase you learn exactly what is known about the problem and what is unknown, select one or more metrics in the process, map the process, make the necessary accurate and sufficient measurements, and record the results to establish the current capability—the baseline.

- **Analyze.** The purpose of the Analyze phase is to sort through all the potential Xs that are causing the costly defects. It's like inputting all the Xs through a funnel so that the resulting output is the vital few Xs that are causing the defects versus the trivial many.

- **Improve.** The purpose of the Improve phase is to create the mathematical relationship of the input Xs to the output of the process to eliminate defects. The objective is to optimize the vital few Xs and their interrelationships to predict certainty of the process capability to deliver expected defect-free outputs. If the process is not predictable the probability of a defect will be higher and as a result will be filled with uncertainty and require improvement.

- **Control.** After each phase comes a phase-gate, or tollgate, review. This is a critical checkpoint in which the black belt, team members, master black belt, and champion meet with executive managers. The team members report on their work in the phase they're completing, and the managers have the opportunity to discuss the work, ask

FOCUS ON FACTS

CAUTION

Everything in the Six Sigma world can be reduced to an equation. In other words, no matter what you're looking at or what you think about the way a given process operates, you can develop a statistical analysis that will evaluate its performance in quantifiable terms, free from opinions and emotions. Six Sigma is about facts, not opinions—you can't measure perceptions, but you can evaluate equations!

questions, and make suggestions. The point is to determine whether the team has performed the activities specified for that phase of the project and whether the team has achieved the stated objectives. If all has gone properly, the team is authorized to move on to the next phase.

Like virtually all else you do in Six Sigma, DMAIC involves following the necessary steps in sequence, each of which is essential to achieving the desired outcome. Although there may be some reiteration, you can't skip or jump around with the four or five phases and expect to get credible results. There's no value in starting with Control, for example, and working your way back to Measure or Define. By following each step in the proper order and completing the tasks for each, you can accurately understand, evaluate, and work on all aspects of the CTQ elements in your products, services, and processes.

Manager's Checklist for Chapter 3

☑ As you get started, keep your objectives clear, stay on track, and focus on results.

☑ Make sure all executives regularly communicate why, when, and how you are undertaking Six Sigma projects so that all employees who are involved or affected are committed to your efforts.

☑ Survey people in your organization so you know how much they know about basic Six Sigma tools and can gauge the extent and depth of training they'll need before starting.

☑ Plan your Six Sigma initiative thoroughly. There are many things to organize and many people to prepare and coordinate to ensure the best possible outcomes.

☑ Involve executive managers in leading the Six Sigma initiative and in promoting it throughout the organization. Their leadership is critical to success.

☑ Make sure every champion owns the process in question and is dedicated to doing whatever it takes to make it easier for the black belts to achieve results.

☑ Understand and define key operational roles from the start. Make sure that all the key players know their responsibilities and how all the roles work together.

☑ Choose an outside consultant with the demonstrated qualifications your organization needs to lead your Six Sigma initiative.

☑ Understand the purpose of each of the five Six Sigma phases— Define, Measure, Analyze, Improve, and Control.

Define Phase

The secret of success is constancy of purpose.
—Benjamin Disraeli (1804–1881)

The purpose of the Define phase is to determine the project's purpose, objectives, and scope, to collect information on the customers and the process involved, and to specify the project deliverables to internal and external customers.

The Define phase starts the process improvement project by addressing these questions:

- What is the problem we need to focus on?
- Who are the customers affected by the problem?
- Which factors are critical to the customers and the processes involved?
- What are the processes involved in the problem?
- Which factors are critical to the processes?
- What is our goal?
- What is our timeline for achieving our goal?

Define Phase Activities

The Define phase consists of these steps.

- Select the champion and identify the process owner.
- Initiate the project charter.

KEY TERM

Project scope Statement that specifies what is included and possibly what is not included in a project and defines the project's boundaries. The scope might include:

- start and stop time;
- duration;
- process boundaries (what is within scope and what is out of scope);
- subprocesses included;
- products or services; and
- divisions and/or locations.

- Form the project team.
- Identify the customers and collect customer data.
- Define the customer CTQ requirements.
- Determine the scope of the project.
- Define and map the core business process—the project focus.
- Establish the project metrics.
- Identify the important problems in the process.
- Develop the problem statement(s) and the business case.
- Focus on the vital few factors.
- Identify the resources necessary.
- Obtain approval for the project.
- Train the team members.
- Form a project plan.
- Conduct the Define phase-gate review.

This outline is generic; the first few steps depend on how an executive team chooses to start a project, and the remaining steps depend on how the champion and the black belt decide to modify the model to suit the specific project.

Determine the Project Selection Strategy and Criteria and Select the Projects

When the Six Sigma initiative is announced, managers at all levels should think about criteria for selecting projects and potential projects. It's generally best to gather as many ideas for projects as possible, so it's smart to encourage ideas from everyone in the organization at every level and in every area.

The organization's executive team, whether it's of the entire company, or a division or business unit, is usually responsible for determining the strategy for selecting projects and the criteria to be used. The executive team then selects projects according to the selection criteria, generally with input and guidance from the master black belt. Then the team generates a rough draft of the business case for each project, giving reasons for why time and other resources should be invested in the projects.

The managers should be familiar enough with their processes to identify the chronic issues that your Six Sigma teams should investigate and improve. Your outside consultant should help the executive team select projects that will have a high impact on quality and customer satisfaction and will deliver bottom-line savings.

Select the Champion and Identify the Process Owner

When a project has been selected, the executive leadership team chooses the project champion.

As mentioned in Chapter 3, a *champion* is a senior manager responsible for ensuring that resources are available for Six Sigma training and the process improvement project and for using his or her authority to overcome barriers—functional, financial, personal, etc.—so that black belts can do their work. The champion is ultimately responsible for project results. The champion is usually drawn from the ranks of the executives and managers. He or she should have enough authority or influence to provide resources and remove obstacles without needing to go higher in the organization.

The executive leadership team also identifies the process owner and involves him or her immediately. The *process owner,* or *sponsor,* is the person with authority over how a process operates, the ultimate responsibility for the results, and the authority to sign off on changes to the process—usually the manager for the area in which the process is located. The process owner may also be the project champion.

> **Process owner** Person with authority over how a process operates, the ultimate responsibility for the results, and the authority to sign off on changes to the process. Also known as the *sponsor.*
>
> **KEY TERM**

Develop the Project Charter

The project charter is dynamic: It starts when the project starts, is developed during the Define phase, and continues to evolve throughout the project. The project charter officially establishes the project and the project team; it sets a direction and objectives.

The project charter documents the:

- project team members;
- problem statement;
- business case;
- objectives;
- stakeholders;
- scope;
- resources and authorization; and
- target completion date for each phase.

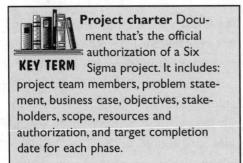

Project charter Document that's the official authorization of a Six **KEY TERM** Sigma project. It includes: project team members, problem statement, business case, objectives, stakeholders, scope, resources and authorization, and target completion date for each phase.

The project charter actually starts unofficially when the executive team defines the project and roughs out a business case for it. Then, when the champion is appointed, he or she usually drafts the charter, listing at minimum the team members and their roles and responsibilities, setting the project objectives and linking them to the organization's objectives, and creating the project rationale or justification. When a black belt is chosen to lead the team, he or she reviews and clarifies the project rationale with the champion.

Figure 4-1 shows the elements of a project charter. At this point, the charter contains little information. Throughout the Define phase, the team members add information to the charter and modify it.

Most of the elements of a project charter are easy to understand. We discuss a few of the more substantive elements later in this chapter.

One point should be made here about the project title. It's important to give the project a title that describes it accurately so others can understand at a glance the project focus and purpose. That may not seem

Project Charter	
Project Name:	
Black Belt Name:	Champion Name:
Project Start Date:	Project Location:
Project Complete Date:	
Business Case:	
Problem Statement:	
Problem Objective:	
Team Members:	
Stakeholders:	
Subject Matter Experts:	
Constraints/Assumptions	
Scope Start Point:	
Scope End Point:	
Preliminary Plan: (attach to this form)	
Black Belt Sign-off:	
Champion Sign-off:	

Figure 4-1. Sample format of a project charter

important when the project starts or throughout the life of the project. But after it ends, others may want to use the project reports as a guide or as a source of lessons learned. The name should make it easy for them to know what they are likely to find in the project reports.

When listing the subject matter experts, it may be useful to indicate after each name the area of expertise, especially if the team is cross-functional and the members don't know each other or if there are subject matter experts who are not assigned to the project team.

The charter is the official project and project team documentation; it authorizes the champion and the team to use organizational resources for the project and forms the basis of communication with stakeholders. It should provide all the information necessary for anyone in the organization to understand the basic facts of the project—what, who, when, where, how, and (especially) why.

In some organizations, it's useful to create a team charter as well. Although team charter is sometimes used synonymously with project charter, a team charter is the document that authorizes each team member to work on that team. That charter should detail when the team will meet and for how long the members need to be released from their regular jobs. The managers of the departments from which the members are selected then sign off on the team charter, acknowledging and approving the partial loan of their employees.

Form the Project Team

The project champion and black belt then choose the employees to become their team members. A project team typically consists of five to eight people and generally no more than a dozen.

The members should be chosen according to the project's specific needs, of course, including green belts and people with knowledge of the process. If possible, there should be a range or balance of personality types.

Identify the Customers

The black belt and team members should identify the customers of the process, as defined in Chapter 2: any persons, groups, or things that are recipients of any input of a process. This step is essential for making smart decisions about how the team can collect customer data and identify the customers' specific CTQ requirements. The team must identify all customer segments, especially those most concerned with the project.

A SIPOC (Supplies, Inputs, Process, Outputs, Customers) diagram, introduced in Chapter 2, is a good tool for identifying customers of a process as well as for understanding the project boundaries and scope. Under the last of the five headings—Customers—the team lists all the customers (the recipients of the process outputs).

Identifying customers may seem easy, but a common mistake occurs when project teams fail to identify all the people who could help them amass customer data. For example, there may be employees who work with external customers such as in sales and marketing or handling complaints who have useful customer insights.

Collect Customer Data

As the team members identify the customers of the process, the team must determine what information it needs to collect to understand what the customers expect or require from the process—the Voice of the Customer (VOC).

The team should start with information already available within the organization. This may be reactive, coming from customer complaints, service calls, product returns, warranty claims, and so on. It may also have been gathered proactively by others in the company. This information is easy to obtain, but it may be outdated and it certainly won't answer all the questions the team should be asking about the process.

To supplement this information and fill in the gaps, the team must go after the VOC proactively. There are several ways to obtain information (such as surveys, customer interviews, focus groups, comment cards, information gathered by sales reps visiting customers, and market research), so the team must determine exactly what information is needed and the most appropriate ways to get it. A good plan for collecting customer data should include:

- a brief description of the project;
- the customer groups targeted;
- the specific data needed;
- operational definitions of potentially ambiguous words;
- the reason(s) for collecting the data; and
- how the team will analyze the data.

Define the Customer CTQ Requirements

The next step is for the team to translate the VOC information into measurable critical-to-quality requirements that it can use as goals for the process improvements. Translating VOC needs into CTQs consists of three basic steps.

FINDING AFFINITY

Affinity diagram Tool used to organize data into categories. To create an affinity diagram:

1. Write each customer statement of need on an index card or self-stick note.
2. Randomly place the cards/notes on a table or attach to a wall.
3. Sort the cards or notes into thematic groups.
4. Create a statement for each group to serve as a "header."

TOOLS

1. Organize the VOC needs into groups. A good tool for doing this is an affinity diagram (see Tools sidebar for a definition). Summarize each group with a succinct statement of the type of needs.
2. Use the VOC needs within each group to show the factors for each type of need, the factors that constitute what the customers mean by "quality," called the "quality drivers." A CTQ tree (Figure 4-2) is a good, simple way to organize the needs and component factors.
3. Break down each quality driver into increasingly specific descriptions, until the each factor has been translated into actionable metrics. What is the minimum requirement for each CTQ to satisfy the customers?

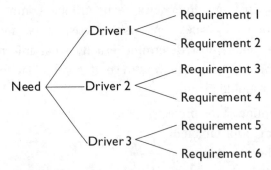

Figure 4-2. CTQ tree

The team can prioritize the CTQ requirements according to the number of VOC comments concerning each quality driver. If possible, the team should enlist the customers in prioritizing the requirements. The team can supply the customers with a list of drivers to rank in order of importance (e.g., from 1–5). You need to know the relative importance of each CTQ requirement so you can focus on what matters most and so you have the basis for making any trade-off decisions that arise later in the project.

Here are two examples, with definitions of defect, unit, and opportunity (explained in Chapter 2):

> **Customer Service Call Center**
> Customer Quote: "I always wait too long to talk to someone."
> Category of CTQ Need: CS Rep Responsiveness
> CTQ Metric: Seconds waiting for rep
> CTQ Requirement: Less than 60 seconds from call connect to automated response system
> Defect: Hold time of 60 seconds or longer
> Unit: Call
> Opportunity: 1 per call
>
> **Magazine Publisher**
> Customer Quote: "I can't tolerate typos."
> Category of CTQ Need: Typographic Quality
> CTQ Metric: Number of typos
> CTQ Requirement: Zero typos
> Defect: Any typo
> Unit: Magazine issue
> Opportunity: Words per magazine issue

Determine the Project Scope

Project scope refers to the boundaries within which the Six Sigma team works. The black belt and the champion, with the help of the master black belt, decide what the team should and should not be doing. In a way, project scope is synonymous with project definition.

Scoping ensures that the team will focus on the biggest problem, the best opportunity for improvement. When scoping a project, those involved should understand where they could gain the greatest financial benefits.

One way to do this is to use a Pareto chart (Figure 4-3). This bar chart displays the relative importance of items—in this case, problem areas and the impact of each—and tracks the cumulative effect of the items. The team can use the chart to identify the areas where the project could achieve the greatest impact. It then must decide how much it can handle within the project. The team may not be able to attack all the most important areas, but it could hit four of the seven greatest problems, for example, which could amount to 70 percent of the cost of the problem. It's better to scope properly and achieve 70 percent of the benefits than to

scope too widely or too vaguely to chase after 100 percent of the benefits
and then fail.

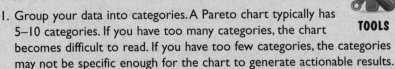

PARETO CHART

A *Pareto chart* is a bar chart that displays the relative importance
of items and tracks the cumulative effect of each.

TOOLS

1. Group your data into categories. A Pareto chart typically has
   5–10 categories. If you have too many categories, the chart
   becomes difficult to read. If you have too few categories, the categories
   may not be specific enough for the chart to generate actionable results.
2. Arrange the bars (1 bar = 1 data category) from left to right, starting
   with the category containing the most data (often the number of
   defects of a given type) and continuing in descending order. Label each
   bar along the X-axis and indicate above the bar its percentage of the
   total number (e.g., 10% of all defects).
3. Draw a Y-axis along the left side and mark increments for the number
   of data values.
4. Draw another Y-axis along the right side and mark increments from
   0–100%.
5. Draw a line from the top of the first bar over the other bars to indicate
   the cumulative percent.

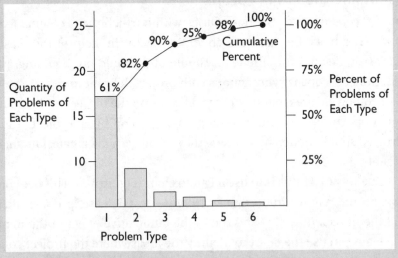

Figure 4-3. Sample Pareto Chart

Back to the charter: The black belt, the champion, and the master
black belt must set the project's boundaries and its start and stop points.

This is an important part of the charter, because it sets limits by specifying what will and won't be included in the project. The team should seek a balance between ambition and reality. It's great to want to take make the biggest gains possible, but it's necessary to finish the project within six months or so.

Determining the scope from the start helps the team avoid "scope creep"—the all-too-natural tendency for team members to attempt a little more, to change direction slightly, or to avoid a situation that turns out to be more problematic than expected. Scope creep can undermine a project and even cause it to fail.

Scope creep Tendency of project team members to expand their project beyond the specified **KEY TERM** parameter, to include more processes, activities, and/or tasks. Scope creep can occur when the project scope is improperly or poorly defined, documented, and controlled. Scope creep results in increased time, human resources, and costs.

The champion is responsible for ensuring that scope creep does not happen. The objective is to have a narrow focus, typically one or two outputs (Ys)—and no more.

JUST SAY NO!
In training black belt candidates, I usually start by urging them to focus on the project as defined. Most employees selected to **CAUTION** become black belts are very capable in technical matters and project management. However, in beginning the Six Sigma journey, the black belts in training are transitioning from their old jobs. To avoid distractions, they must be able to say *no!* to outside project requests, including tasks of their old jobs. Part of the success model of Six Sigma is getting a strong black belt to focus his or her full-time attention on the defined project.

Here's a real example of scope creep in a Six Sigma project I was involved with about a decade ago. The project focus was a specific defect type called inventory forecasting accuracy and the focus was North America. However, in the first couple weeks of the project, we found other defects, including some in Europe—service levels of specific SKUs, an out-of-control sales "giveaway program," warranty returns going back to

SMART

MANAGING

KEY TO MAINTAINING FOCUS
Steve Jobs, entrepreneur and cofounder of Apple, once offered some words of wisdom about innovation that apply perfectly to the scope of process improvement projects: "People think focus means saying yes to the thing you've got to focus on. But that's not what it means at all. It means saying no to the hundred other good ideas."

the distribution center out of control and at random, and local plants out of compliance with the central forecasting. The actual IT forecasting application defaults were not set and IT was possibly going to change software in the middle of the project.

The result was chaos, confusion, a lack of focus, a discouraged new black belt candidate, and no action items toward any solution. What was the focus of the project now? Was the black belt now responsible for working not only on the service level but also on all the other possible measurable outputs?

After a while, the project was five weeks behind schedule, we had made no progress, and the black belt candidate was confused and frustrated. To get the project on track, we returned to the original project definition, and some of the findings became Xs that were the cause of the problem. The original focus was North America, the primary metric was forecast accuracy as measured in percent of a ±25 percent goal, and the secondary metric was service levels in order to keep the primary metric in check—and that was it!

How do you minimize scope creep? Here are four recommendations:

1. The black belt must spend enough time up front with the appropriate subject matter experts to initialize the scope, typically one or two days.
2. The champion should focus the scope using a project prioritization matrix (see the example in Figure 4-4).
3. The champion must ask "in-scope" and "out-of-scope" questions (i.e., Is this within our scope or outside our scope?) about defect type, location-specific framing, and other issues. There must be agreement among top management.
4. To keep everyone focused, the black belt, the team members, and

the champion must constantly refer to the project definition. The black belt and the champion must not allow scope creep or at least must agree to minimize the possible damage.

Use any tendency toward scope creep to good advantage. If team members want to add an issue or an area to the project definition, consider documenting the suggestion for possible addition to the list of high-potential projects you should be keeping for the future.

	Project Selection Criteria and Significance Ratings Potential Projects and Impact Rating	Direct links to strategic goals	Relates to key business/process (Objectives)	Customer satisfaction impact	Data availability	Measurable	Increasing revenue/financial payback/Cost takeout	ROI	Project scope/complexity-cross/single function	Time to resolve problem	Ease of quantification of financial impact	Employee satisfaction impact	Specific need to improve	Resource availability (time, people, capital)	Overall (sum of the columns)
	Significance Ratings														
1	No End Trim	8	6	3	5	8	8	5	4	3	5	4	7	4	69
2	Length Variation	8	8	5	4	8	8	5	4	3	5	4	7	5	74
3	Braze Rework	10	10	4	6	9	4	4	10	4	6	9	9	4	89
4	Plating European	9	10	4	4	3	6	4	2	2	3	3	4	9	66
5															
6															
	Scoring: Multiply potential projects and impact rating column times Significance Ratings														
Notes:															

Significance ratings set by senior management 1 = Low; 10 = Very High.
Select potential projects with highest rating.
Potential impact rating determined by impact of the potential projects to criteria. See Scoring Matrix. Projects without "data availability" cannot move forward without discussion.

Figure 4-4. Sample project prioritization matrix

If the project scope seems too large, the team should recommend a plan for splitting it into two or more smaller projects of realistic scope, to be worked simultaneously or in succession. It may be possible, for example, to break a large project into a black belt project and one or more smaller projects to be led by green belts.

Scoping also allows the black belt and the champion to identify the resources and the skills the project will require and to sketch out a time frame for completing the project.

PRIORITIZATION MATRIX

Use a prioritization matrix (also known as a *criteria matrix* or *decision matrix*) to rate a set of items (e.g., projects, problems, tasks, issues) by importance based on criteria that are weighted by significance.

TOOLS

1. Determine criteria for assessing importance (typically 6–12 items). List them across the top of the chart as column headings.
2. Assign each criterion a number according to its relative significance.
3. Create a numerical rating scale of the projects (e.g., 1–10).
4. List the items down the left of the chart.
5. Rate each project according to each criterion, using the rating scale.
6. Multiply the rating for each criterion by its weight and record the score.
7. Add the scores for each item and record the total in the final column.

(Sometimes the criteria are listed down the left and the items across the top.)

Here are some suggestions for scoping Six Sigma projects:

- Know about other projects or activities that might affect the project.
- Clarify project expectations. Make sure that they are aligned, so they don't pull the team in different directions.
- Focus on finances. The chances for success are better if the financial benefits are carefully quantified from the start.
- Differentiate between soft (subjective) and hard (objective) metrics.
- Don't cross boundaries. If a project has more than one owner, conflicts and problems may arise.
- Keep time in mind. If a project cannot be delimited sufficiently to fit into a four- to-six-month time frame, it may be necessary to break it into smaller projects.
- Write a precise and concise scope statement—an "elevator speech." The more easily project team members can grasp the scope, the easier it is for them to focus on the project and to communicate about it with each other and people outside the project.

Define and Map the Core Business Process— the Project Focus

The team should know the start and end points of the process if they have been set. If not, the team should set them.

Next, between those two points, the team maps the more important steps in the process. This should be a high-level map or flowchart of the sequence of activities, a further development of the SIPOC diagram, the first of several process maps the team will create.

Establish the Project Metrics

After the team has translated the VOC data from "customer language" into customer CTQ requirements, it must choose the measures by which it will assess progress toward meeting those requirements, throughout the project and, ultimately, at the end. It should be relatively easy to derive the metrics from the CTQs. The project metrics (distinct from process metrics, which are determined in the Measure phase) are basically the CTQ specifications.

Selecting project metrics is one of the crucial elements of the charter. Project metrics should reflect the VOC, of course, but they should also reflect the voice of the business—its stated mission, goals, and objectives and its unstated needs or requirements. When selecting metrics, the project team should consider how the metrics relate to key business metrics.

Team members should specify all the metrics that they think may be relevant, but the metrics must be within the project scope. Metrics generally relate to any of three basic dimensions—quality, time (cycle or delivery time), and money (cost or price). In Six Sigma terminology, metrics for these dimensions are critical to quality (CTQ), critical to delivery (CTD), and critical to price (CTP).

The project metrics should be simple, straightforward, and meaningful—they must help team members, whatever their functional area, understand how the process is performing in such a way that everyone shares the same understanding. Good examples would be cost of poor quality (COPQ) and rolled throughput yield (RTY).

The team should review its metrics with the executive team to ensure the metrics align with the organization's strategies and objectives.

Identify the Important Problems in the Process

The team has identified the customer CTQs. Now it identifies and quantifies process outputs that don't meet those requirements. Which process outputs aren't meeting customer CTQs and in what ways? How extensive

KEY TERMS

Cost of poor quality (COPQ) Calculation of any costs that would not be incurred if quality were perfect. These costs can be for internal failures (e.g., scrap, rework, reinspection, process changes), external failures (e.g., returns, warranty claims, loss of revenue, fees and penalties), inspection and evaluation (e.g., inspections, tests), and prevention (e.g., quality planning, process control, process audits).

Rolled throughput yield (RTY) Calculation of the probability that a unit can pass through a process without defects. It is the product of the first-pass yields at each step.

To calculate the RTY, calculate the first-pass yield for each process step and multiply all the yields.

is the problem? How many outputs are defective? How far are the defective outputs from meeting CTQ requirements? How often are the outputs defective?

For each problem identified, the team should assess its importance to the customers. A good measure might be in the relative importance of the CTQs and in the extent of the defects.

The team should also assess the importance of each problem to the company. As noted above, two good measures would be the COPQ and RTY.

Develop the Problem Statement(s) and the Business Case

After identifying the problem, the team develops a statement for each problem (or opportunity for improvement) in the process. Creating a good problem statement, also known as a project statement, can take a lot of thought and work. It must be specific in defining and quantifying the problem; otherwise, it's difficult to set meaningful goals, establish good metrics, focus efforts, measure progress, and show the results of the project in terms that matter. The experience of Six Sigma practitioners suggests that about 80 percent of projects that fail are doomed from the beginning because they are improperly defined.

The problem statement should define the problem area objectively, specifically, and concisely. It should include the basic facts, such as the circumstances in which the problem occurs and the extent of the problem's impact. The statement should focus on observable symptoms and not suggest possible causes or, certainly, imply blame.

Developing a good problem statement is critical to communicating and directing your project mission.

Here's an example of a good problem statement: "Product returns are 5% of sales, resulting in a profit impact of $5 million and customer dissatisfaction rates in excess of 50%." The statement is specific: It presents numbers that represent the extent of the problem and it indicates the core cost and customer satisfaction issues.

In contrast, here's an example of a poor problem statement: "Our product return levels are too high due to product A and will be reduced by analyzing first- and second-level Pareto charts." This problem statement is poor for two reasons. First, there are no numbers, so there's no quantifying the scope or scale of the problem. Second, it states only what you're going to do, instead of precisely and accurately quantifying the effects of the problem.

The problem statement should also provide a baseline, set improvement goals, indicate the approach for resolving the problem, sketch a time frame for the project, and estimate the benefits and financial savings to the organization—the opportunity in resolving the problem.

Baseline Measurement of the current state of the process before making changes. The baseline becomes the standard against which any improvement is measured.

The baseline used in the Define phase to make the business **KEY TERM** case for the project is a primary business measure, such as cost to produce a product or provide a service, cycle time, RTY, or COPQ.
During the Measure phase, baselines are established for process characteristics or process performance, such as capabilities for each CTQ.

This is also known as making the business case for the project, developing the case made by the executive team when it generated and evaluated project ideas. The purpose of developing the business case is to identify and quantify all potential benefits of committing time and other resources to the project and modifying the problematic processes. The business case should be compelling to the executive managers. Otherwise, the project may be dropped before it gets through the Define phase.

The problem statement should be clear, concise, and specific.

Any problem statement must include information that would answer these questions:

- What's the problem? Which process outputs don't meet customer CTQs and in what ways?
- Where does the problem occur? In what area(s) of the process?
- How extensive is the problem? How many outputs are defective? How far are the defective outputs from meeting CTQ requirements? How often are the outputs defective? Are there any trends?
- Why is it important to solve this problem? How important is this problem to customers and the organization?

A problem statement should *not* include the causes of the problem, only the effects.

A problem statement should *not* include actions likely to solve the problem, only the need to find a solution.

A good problem statement:

- Creates a sense of ownership for the team;
- Helps the team focus and reduces the chances for scope creep; and
- Presents the effects of the problem in measurable terms.

The business case communicates the need for the project in terms of meeting business objectives. It consists of the:

- Output unit (product/service) for external customers;
- Primary business measure of output unit for the project;
- Baseline performance of the primary business measure; and
- Gap in baseline performance of the primary business measure from the business objectives.

Figure 4-5 will help the champion and black belt with the executive team draft a script to make a business case and define the problem statement.

Figure 4-6 shows an example of the template for a payment process project.

Notice that the quantification and specific time have been leveraged to demonstrate the business case.

Know your business case type:

Fill in the Blanks for Your Project

During _____, the _____ for
    (period of time for baseline performance)   (primary business measure)

_____ was _____.The gap of _____
 (a key business process)   (baseline performance)   (business objective target vs. baseline)

from _____ represents _____ of cost impact.
   (business objective)   (cost impact of gap)

Figure 4-5. Template for making a business case and defining the problem

During <u>the first half of 2015 (Jan-Jun), the Actual vs. Budget Index</u> for
   (period of time for baseline performance)   (primary business measure)

<u>payment processing</u> was <u>−1.75.</u> The gap of <u>1.86 index points</u>
(a key business process)   (baseline performance)   (business objective target vs baseline)

From <u>+0.11</u> represents <u>$185,000</u> of cost impact.
(business objective)   (cost impact of gap)

Index = Budget − Actual ÷ Budget

	Expense ($000)	Difference from Budget f/(u)	Performance Index f/(u)
Actual	275	(175)	(1.75)
Budget	100		—
Target	90	10	0.11
Index Points from Target f/(u)			(1.86)

Figure 4-6. Template for a payment process project

- Priority 1 projects directly impact the income or cash flow statement.
- Priority 2 projects impact the balance sheet (working capital).
- Priority 3 projects avoid expenses (or investments) due to known or expected events in the future.
- Priority 4 projects are risk management/insurance projects that prevent unpredictable events or reduce their severity. Creating the ability to capitalize on market opportunities may also fall into this category.

You may have a combination of types.

As mentioned above, the baseline used to make the business case is a measurement of the current status of the process using one or more key metrics such as the cost for the process to produce a certain product or provide a certain service, the cycle time, the RTY, or the COPQ.

> **Entitlement** Best performance that can be reasonably
> expected from a process.
>   It can also be defined as:
>
>
> **KEY TERM**
>
> ■ The top performance achieved in the span of a certain
>   period, the best documented level of performance;
> ■ The best potential performance of a process, based on the current
>   design; or
> ■ The best performance possible under ideal conditions.

> **DEFINING ENTITLEMENT ON THE JOB**
> **FOR EXAMPLE**
> "We defined entitlement as the average of the best three con-
> secutive data points operating under normal conditions while in
> statistical control. The theory was that if your process ran there
> for three consecutive periods without modifications or improve-
> ments, it should be capable of running there consistently under optimal
> conditions once the factors influencing the outputs are identified and con-
> trolled."
> —Comment posted to an online Six Sigma forum

The improvement goals should address those metrics, estimating improvement in terms of percentages and dollars saved. The team should calculate the performance gap, the difference between the baseline and the *entitlement* (defined as the best performance that can be reasonably expected from the process). A *goal* is the portion of that gap the project team is trying to capture.

What results does the team anticipate from this project? To reduce defects by at least 85 percent? To reduce cycle time by 45 percent? To identify variable costs and limit them to $75 per transaction?

The team should set challenging yet realistic goals. It should also indicate what it plans to do to achieve those goals and when it expects to achieve them. This information should be included in a preliminary proj-ect plan that the black belt develops further after the executive team approves the project and allocates the resources.

To give an estimate of the benefits and financial savings to the organ-ization, the team should perform a cost-benefit analysis. To do so, the team must ascertain the cost of poor quality. It's as easy or as difficult as quantifying the waste in the process. If the process is producing scrap, quantify the cost of the scrap. If it's causing rework, quantify the cost of the rework. If employees are spending time in non-value-added activities in the process or because of it, quantify the cost of those nonvalue-added activities. After estimating the cost of poor quality, the team should estimate the cost of resources to do the project. Then it can make the business case by calculating the ROI.

The problem statement has two purposes:

- To focus the team on the problem(s) in the process and
- To communicate the purpose of the project to the executive team.

The problem statement should answer the following questions for the executive team:

- What's the problem?
- What's the status of this process?
- What do we need to do to change the process?
- How long will it take to make the changes?
- What will be the cost of the resources required?
- How much money will the changes save?

The problem statement should be objective, specific, and concise, as stated above, and it should also be compelling. The project team should keep in mind that it's answering this pair of related questions:

- Why are we doing this project now?
- What negative consequences will result if we don't do this project now?

In other words, the problem statement should make a case for the importance and urgency of the project.

Include the problem statement(s) and the business case with the project charter.

From the problem statement, the black belt can further develop the preliminary project plan. In consultation with the master black belt and the champion, the black belt adds to the preliminary plan the training that he or she and the team members will need throughout the project.

Focus on the Vital Few Factors

A term commonly used in Six Sigma, "vital few" was coined by Joseph M. Juran, in contrast with the "trivial many" (although in later years he pre-

Pareto Principle Theory that posits that for many phenomena, 80 percent of the effects stem from 20 percent of the causes. Also called 80/20 Rule and Pareto's Law.

KEY TERM

ferred "useful many"). Juran derived this concept from studying the work of Vilfredo Pareto, after whom he named the *Pareto Principle*, also known as the *80/20 Rule*, which posits that, for many events, roughly 80 percent of the effects result from 20 percent of the causes. A Pareto chart is a good tool for displaying data in categories to identify the problem's vital few components.

Determine the Resources Necessary

At this stage, it's time to determine what resources (e.g., money, administrative support, training) will be needed to carry out the project. The black belt, the champion, and the executive leader should consult with a member of your financial department to identify these resources.

Obtain Project Approval

This step needs no explanation. As with any business project, the champion and/or the team leader takes to the executive leader the project charter, the process map, the business case, the problem statement, and the statement of resources necessary for the project. The executive leader approves the project or may request more information or changes.

Start Training the Team Members

After the project has received approval, the master black belt begins to train the project team members as appropriate for the project and each member's level of Six Sigma knowledge and experience.

Form a Project Plan

It's important to have a project plan, to focus your efforts from the start and to ensure that your project stays focused.

The plan should consist of steps, scheduled milestones, deliverables, and goals for each of the five DMAIC phases. The champion and the black belt work together to create this plan.

Your plan should include these components:

- **Milestones.** Checkpoints that indicate when and where the team should be in the project. At each milestone the black belt reports to the champion on the team's progress and any problems encountered.
- **Deliverables.** Things to be completed by the end of the phase (phase-gate review).
- **Tasks.** Include the person designated to have primary responsibility for each task and the tools to be used.
- **Communications plan.** This should specify:
  - the items to be communicated (such as project status reports, minutes of team meetings, etc.);
  - the person who will communicate each item (champion, black belt, green belt, or other person);
  - the people to whom each item will be communicated (team members, executive leaders, or others);
  - when or how frequently the information is communicated;
  - how the information is communicated (memo, e-mail, phone call, presentation, etc.); and
  - where the information communicated will be stored for future reference.

Define the Phase-Gate Review

As mentioned in Chapter 3, each of the five DMAIC phases ends with a review to determine whether the project team has performed the activities specified for that phase in the plan and achieved the stated objectives. At the end of the Define phase, these are among the basic questions to consider:

- Has the project charter been modified? If so, how?
- Is there sufficient evidence to support the business case made for the project in the charter?
- Are there problems yet to be resolved?
- Does the team face any barriers?
- What does the team plan to do during the Measure phase?

If the executive team decides the project team has completed the Define phase successfully, it authorizes the team to move on to the Measure phase.

Summary

The purpose of the Define phase is to determine the purpose, objectives, and scope of the project; to collect information on the customers and the process involved; and to specify the project deliverables to the customers (internal and external). You identify the important problems in your processes and determine the vital few factors to be measured, analyzed, improved, and controlled in the remaining four phases of the Six Sigma methodology.

Manager's Checklist for Chapter 4

☑ Your project charter authorizes a Six Sigma project. The charter should include a list of project team members, problem statement, business case, objectives, stakeholders, scope, resources and authorization, and target completion date for each phase.

☑ Be cautious about adding to the project as defined and authorized in the charter to avoid scope creep and ensure that the team members stay true to the project's initial intent.

☑ The people involved in scoping a project should understand where they could gain the greatest financial benefits for the organization.

☑ The improvement goals should include specific financial goals, with estimates in terms of percentages and dollars saved.

☑ Six Sigma training should start for team members as soon as the resources have been approved.

☑ At the end of the Define phase, the project team should have:
- the project charter;
- a high-level process map;
- a VOC analysis, with CTQ metrics and requirements;
- problem statements;
- a project management plan, including milestones, deliverables for each phase, task (with person responsible and tools to be used), and communications plan; and
- the resources identified and authorized.

Measure Phase

I often say that when you can measure what you are speaking about and express it in numbers, you know something about it; but when you cannot measure it, when you cannot express it in numbers, your knowledge is of a meagre and unsatisfactory kind.

—William Thomson, Lord Kelvin (1824–1907)

We don't know what we don't know. We can't act on what we don't know. We won't know until we search. We won't search for what we don't question. We don't question what we don't measure."

—Dr. Mikel Harry

The purpose of the Measure phase is *not* to solve the problem. It's to understand exactly where you are, what you know, and what you don't know. We're exploring the output of the problem, called the Ys. We start by listing potential causes of the problem, called the Xs. This problem-solving journey comes not in the Define phase, but begins in the Measure phase.

The objective for the project team members is to ensure that the data they use are validated using specific tools. Concurrently, they select one or more metrics in the process (i.e., Ys, or dependent variables), mapping the process, taking the necessary measurements, and recording the results to establish the current capability, or baseline. The focus is on recording accurate and sufficient measurements of the process. The team creates sampling plans to ensure sufficient size, frequency of collection, and a rational subgroup that represents the process realistically.

Question: What does Six Sigma need? Answer: It needs five things:

1. a problem;
2. a process;
3. a financial benefit;
4. a metric and a goal; and
5. a customer metric.

In the Measure phase we quantify, qualify, and validate those Six Sigma needs. We normally don't find solutions, but we do discover more opportunities and lay a foundation for the culture to follow. Measurement is the stage during which struggles occur and barriers emerge.

The black belts and their efforts invariably run up against cultural resistance. Although our strategy and deployment prepare people in the organization for the cultural change, in the Measure phase "the rubber meets the road." It would be naïve to expect people to jump for joy when you ask them to install a system that will inevitably reveal detailed information that will be used to attack core practices or undermine people's beliefs and authorities and will change the definitions of success and failure. Managers and employees often view Six Sigma as a threat to their job security.

During the Measure phase, processes are examined. It may seem as if the situation is getting worse, since defects will increase as the real levels of the defect rates are uncovered. Once these improvement opportunities are exposed, the team members must redefine the problem to reflect what they learn about the defects and their true costs. They search for root causes by measuring the process to determine the focus and extent of the problem and using data to identify the major factors or vital few root causes.

Purposes of the Measure Phase

In the Measure phase the team focuses the improvement effort by gathering information about the current situation. This helps the team narrow the range of potential causes it needs to investigate in the Analyze phase. The other goals of this phase are to:

■ Define one or more CTQ characteristics (dependent variables);

- Map the process in detail;
- Evaluate the measurement systems;
- Assess the current level of process performance to establish a baseline capability and the short- and long-term process sigma capabilities; and
- Quantify the problem.

Measure Phase Activities

Figure 5-1 shows a detailed map of the Measure phase activities. Note the extent of the team's involvement in this phase. This is where the team facilitation tools learned in the Define phase are especially important.

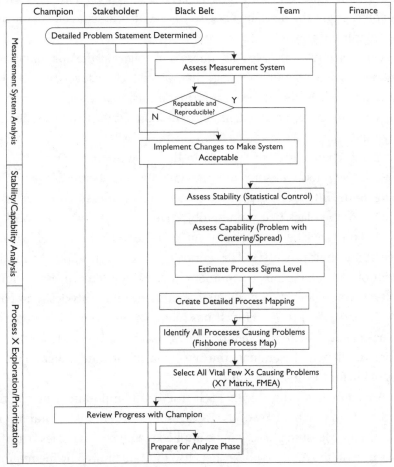

Figure 5-1. Map of the Measure phase

This flowchart lays out a general guide for using the tools. There are times when the sequence is not followed. The usual sequence is:

- process map;
- cause-and-effect (fishbone) diagram;
- YX matrix; then
- FMEA.

In a perfect world, we would also expect measurement system analysis (MSA) to precede capability.

In many cases—and this is especially true for projects about transactional processes—the black belt must first establish a data collection system. Then, while the team is collecting enough data to perform a capability study, the black belt begins to execute the sequence of tools in the order listed above.

One objective of the Measure phase is to collect all the qualitative and experiential information possible, then objectively categorize and rank the importance of the pieces of information using tools such as process maps, Pareto charts, and YX diagrams. Additionally, the team uses quantitative and statistical tools to develop a list of possible process inputs (Xs) that it will characterize statistically in the Analyze phase. One group of tools, the MSA tools, ensures that the data the black belt uses are appropriate for the intended purpose. The MSA assesses measurement error.

One of the black belt training objectives in the Measure phase is to instill in the black belts a curiosity and a desire to learn as much as possible about their processes. This curiosity, particularly applied with the intent of controlling the environment and making the process perform better, is contagious. When the team members adopt this desire to constantly learn, then the black belt has made an important first step as a change agent. A team that demonstrates a desire to learn and a sense of curiosity will help disseminate the Six Sigma culture and integrate it as a way of life for the organization.

An ability to synthesize what is learned is an important aspect of the Six Sigma approach. Many of the tools, especially for ranking and prioritizing in the Measure phase, can be applied creatively. This is less true for tools used in the Analyze phase, because they are limited by the requirements of statistical models and assumptions.

Listed here are the most important tools used by the project team in the Measure phase:

1. process mapping;
2. YX diagrams;
3. failure modes and effects analysis (FMEA);
4. measurement systems analysis (MSA); and
5. capability analysis.

Step 1. Map the Process in Detail

The project team starts with the process map, the sequence of steps in the flow of activities that produces goods or provides services. The process map is one of the most important tools. It documents how a process actually works, showing several levels of detail.

The process step and the data surrounding are key to project success. The full characterization *must* be understood at the deep, detailed level. Figure 5-2 shows a simple step in a process of all the top-level parameters—inputs, controls, safety, and outputs—for which the team needs to collect information to make a full characterization of the process.

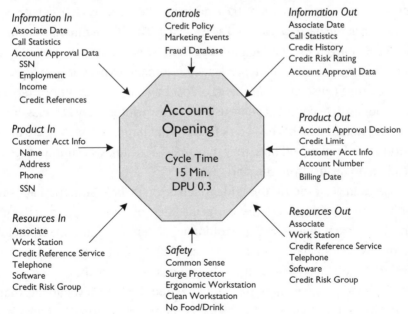

Figure 5-2. Process step detailing the top-level parameters

The team maps the process in detail so it doesn't miss any Xs that could be causing the problem.

For each step in a process, the team must ask and answer two simple but key questions:

1. Why do we do this step?
2. How do we know the result is good?

Let's return to the airline and lost luggage scenario. Step 1 of the baggage-handling process occurs when the check-in agent takes your baggage at the counter and attaches a tag. Question 1: Why do they do this step? Answer: To identify the owner and the destination. Great! Question 2: How do they know that the result is good?

I asked the Delta Airlines agent, "How do you know what you just did is good?"

She answered, "You mean the tag I just put on the luggage?"

"Yes! How do you know the tag you put on the luggage is good?"

"We don't know!"

It was the honest answer. They truly didn't audit the step or measure anything. They just hoped the process would work. But it's not working! It costs an airline an average of $100 to deliver to the owner each bag that does not arrive at the baggage carousel as expected. The airline must also refund the fee it charged for checking the bag. These lost-baggage deliveries cost airlines as much as $8 million per year. And sometimes bags are lost forever.

The root cause of the problem of lost baggage is sharing printers to save money. Two counter agents use the same printer. They get busy, long lines form, and they have to work faster. What happens? As they are both printing and pulling off tags, they may make a mistake, so your luggage is destined to be lost from the start!

Once an error such as this is identified through the DMAIC process, the airline can take the necessary corrective step of investing in a separate printer for each operator. The additional printers will more than pay for themselves within days in savings realized from not routing baggage incorrectly? The lesson is clear: Control the process → Control the outcome!

Detailed process mapping, going beyond the high-level SIPOC map from the Define phase, helps team members think about the process and identify factors that may be causing the problem. Flowcharting software comes in handy when creating process maps, but it's not necessary. PowerPoint is also effective, with the shapes, connectors, and other features accessible through the drawing toolbar.

Process mapping helps a project team:

- Describe how activities are being done;
- Understand the big picture;
- Identify how, when, or where a process should be measured;
- Investigate where problems might occur; and
- Identify where modifications might best be made.

A process map consists of flowcharts of the steps in a process—operations, decision points, delays, movements, handoffs, rework loops, and controls or inspections. Process maps are living documents and must be changed as the process is changed.

Some of the data required for a detailed process map might be unavailable to a team beginning the Measure phase. The team members should document what data are available and determine what data it still needs as it moves into the Analyze phase. The team should quickly set up a system for collecting data wherever it sees that data are needed.

Detailed mapping should be an iterative process as the team learns more about the process. The mapping begins at a high level, with the map created in the Define phase. With this information, the team can determine the most appropriate area on which to focus its investigation to determine more about the process.

Waste

Process maps must identify forms of waste, steps that add no value from the customer's perspective, and points at which the process does not flow smoothly. Figure 5-3 shows a detailed process map that identifies non-value-added steps. The project team should strive to achieve this level of detail.

Seven forms of waste have been identified in the lean enterprise approach to process management (also known as *muda*, the Japanese term). I use an acronym as a way to remember them—DOTWIMP.

1. Defects
2. Overproduction (production or acquisition of items before they're needed)

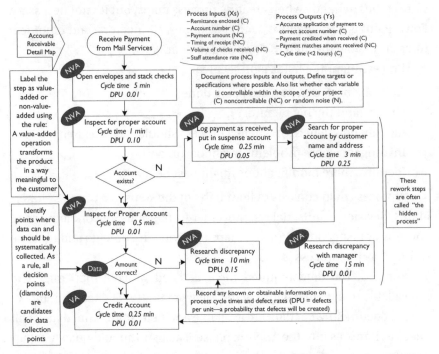

Figure 5-3. Detailed process map with non-value-added steps identified

3. Transportation (moving materials, products, paper, etc., which adds no value for the customer and risks damage, delay, or loss)
4. Waiting (time that employees wait for something they need or to provide goods or services)
5. Inventory (raw materials, work-in-progress, and finished goods represent capital that's not producing income)
6. Motion (movement of employees or equipment)
7. Processing excess or overprocessing (making or doing more than customers need or want)

Step 2. Create a YX Matrix

The YX matrix—also known as YX diagram, XY matrix, cause-and-effect matrix, and house of quality—takes information first identified in the process mapping exercise and then documented through brainstorming methods such as the cause-and-effect (fishbone) diagram. The YX diagram is a way to quantify and prioritize the relationships between input

TRICKS
OF THE
TRADE

MNEMONICS

DOTWIMP may not work for you. Some people prefer other mnemonics. Here are two examples:

TIMWOOD

- T: Transportation
- I: Inventory
- M: Motion
- W: Waiting
- O: Overprocessing
- O: Overproduction
- D: Defect

NOW TIME (now is the time to eliminate waste):

- N: Nonquality (defects)
- O: Overproduction
- W: Waiting
- T: Transportation
- I: Inventory
- M: Motion
- E: Excess processing

variables (Xs) and output variables (Ys). In function and structure, the YX matrix resembles the project prioritization matrix.

The YX matrix is an important team tool, which the team uses to think analytically about the process. This helps facilitate buy-in for the solutions later. The team uses the matrix to collect data for a failure modes and effects analysis (FMEA), discussed next.

YX matrix Way to quantify and prioritize the relationships between input variables (Xs) and output variables (Ys).

KEY TERM

While the YX matrix helps make the analysis of critical inputs and outputs as objective as possible, the source of its information is still team experience and collective wisdom. This is not real data; this is organized brainstorming! The results are not necessarily tied to hard data.

The YX matrix is a team-based tool. The key to success in using the tool is team makeup. Because this tool addresses characteristics of various functional areas, the black belt should consider organizing a cross-functional team for this exercise.

Here are the steps for creating a YX matrix:

1. At a team meeting introduce the concepts of the YX matrix and explain why they are important. Assemble the list of potential Xs from the three sources:
   a. Process mapping (standard, cross-functional, VA/NVA)
   b. Brainstorming (cause-and-effect/fishbone diagram, affinity analysis)
   c. Preliminary data analysis (graphical and statistical)
2. Enter the process name and revision date in the matrix information section.
3. Enter the Ys (primary or secondary) deemed important by the team and/or customers. Use the outputs identified on the process map.
4. Rate each Y from 1 (least important) to 10 (most important) from the customers' perspective.
5. Enter all potential Xs felt to impact Y. Use all the Xs identified in Step 1. This should be comprehensive.
6. Rate the impact of each X on each Y from 1 (least impact) to 10 (greatest impact). At this point it's a "best guess" estimate because no numerical relationships have yet been established.
7. Multiply the impact rating for each X by the importance rating for each Y. Then add the scores for each X and record them in the column at the far right.
8. Analyze the results.

Figure 5-4 shows the basic format of the YX matrix.

The Ys that go in the YX diagram should be those that relate to your metrics. Some people mistakenly enter the Ys for each process step on the map, which are just the Xs for the next step. Start out at a high level. Later you may create a new YX matrix focused on a single step.

The team may find the scoring step to be tedious. Make sure that experts are available who live with the process daily. Consensus is the best decision method to use when scoring these inputs. When the matrix is complete, the team makes sure the results seem reasonable.

The black belt should budget enough time in the team meetings for using this tool, which takes a lot of time. Don't plan to execute a YX matrix in less than 30 minutes; it's not uncommon for this tool to require two

Output Variables (Ys)	Description	1 Payment applied to correct amount	2 Payment matches amount received	3 Interest calculation	4 Available credit calculation	5 Payment posted on time	
	Weight	10	9	6	4	9	
Input Variables (Xs)							Ranking
1	Remittance enclosed	8	7	10	10	8	315
2	Correct account setup	10		9	10	10	284
3	Legibility of remittance	7	9	7	7	6	275
4	Correct send-to address			9	8	10	176
5	Staff attendance	5	5	5	5	8	217
6	Daily volumes	5	5	5	5	8	217
7	Data entry errors	8	10	10	10	8	342
8	Recon report accuracy	2	4	2	2	9	157
9	Recon report availability	2	4	2	2	9	157
10	System uptime	6	5	2	2	10	215
11	Batch processing	8	5			10	195

Figure 5-4. Basic format for the YX matrix

hours or more.

Again, this is a quantification of what the team thinks is most important. It's not based on hard data. This means the results should be treated with some skepticism and they should be verified for logic and reasonableness. The YX matrix will challenge what people believe and will bring out healthy disagreements.

The YX matrix outcome summary (see Figure 5-5 for an example) is used as a priority compass to indicate where to start looking for the factors causing the defect. The tool creates a common dialogue for the team, resulting in a natural team bond against the enemy—the defect!

The focus of this YX matrix summary drives your next steps to focus on the high-priority Xs (input variables) to start measuring and testing the effects of these inputs on the outputs. A side benefit and a key to success

Output Variables	
Description	Weight
Payment applied to correct account	10
Payment matches amount received	9
Payment posted on time	9
Interest calculation	6
Available credit calculation	4

↑
Recap Customer's Priority Weight

"Data entry errors" should be investigated first since it has the highest overall score. This does not mean, however, that data entry actually has the greatest influence on the process. Data Entry Ranking = [(10*8)+(9*10)+ (6*10)+(4*10)+9*8)]

Input Variables	
Description	Input Ranking
Data entry errors	342
Remittance enclosed	315
Correct account setup	284
Legibility of remittance	275
Staff attendance	217
Daily volumes	217
System uptime	215
Batch processing	195
Correct send-to address	176
Recon report accuracy	157
Recon report availability	157

Figure 5-5. Outcome summary of the YX matrix

in using this tool are the deep discussions and, in some cases, the intellectual arguments about the defects that the team will have. The discussions often lead to developing lists of more than a hundred potential Xs.

Step 3. Perform a Failure Modes and Effects Analysis (FMEA)

A failure modes and effects analysis (FMEA) is a technique the project team should adopt to study all possible problems in a process, the potential impact of each problem, and ways to deal with each problem. It's a document that represents the combined knowledge of the process.

The FMEA addresses this question: What do you want to know about a defect? Pause for a minute now to think about a work situation that's a major issue.

OK, do you have something in mind? What do you want to know about the major issue? Make a list of seven major aspects or categories for the major issue. If you tend to solve problems logically, your list will contain at least three items of the FMEA. The FMEA forces questions for which team members must then collect and organize knowledge about the product, process, or service systematically and in a specific format.

> **Failure modes and effects analysis (FMEA)**
> Step-by-step approach to identify all possible ways in **KEY TERM** which a process, product, or service could fail and to prioritize potential failures according to how serious their consequences are, how frequently the failures occur, and how easily the failures can be detected.

The FMEA starts with tribal knowledge (unwritten information known by people close to the process), known defects, and current data collection. Later the team updates the FMEA using data, so that better estimates of detection and occurrence can be obtained. The FMEA is not a tool for identifying the Xs that cause Ys and for eliminating Xs. It's useful for identifying potential Xs and prioritizing them to determine the order in which they should be evaluated.

However, the FMEA isn't a great problem-solving tool and is tremendously challenging to execute in a team environment. (If you thought the YX matrix was tough, try this one!) Used correctly, however, it is the most powerful tool for getting team members to think about the process in ways they've never considered. They will never see processes the same way again. The FMEA is a living document to use as you start to improve: It drives a systematic recordkeeping of the process and drives change through priorities.

There are several types of FMEA, including:

- **System FMEA.** Used to analyze systems and subsystems in the early concept and design stages, focusing on potential failure modes associated with the *functions* of a system caused by *design*.
- **Design FMEA.** Used to analyze products before they're released to production.
- **Process FMEA.** Used to analyze manufacturing and transactional processes.
- **Equipment FMEA.** Used to analyze failure modes in the equipment employed in a process.

Follow these steps when conducting an FMEA:

1. Assign an FMEA number and title to your process.
2. Identify the department responsible for the process and the person responsible for preparing the FMEA.
3. Enter the end customer product name(s).
4. Assign an FMEA key date and an origination date.
5. List the core team members.
6. List the process functions (steps).
7. List the potential failure modes.
8. List the potential failure effects.
9. Assign a severity for each effect.
10. List the potential failure causes.
11. Assign an occurrence level for each cause.
12. List the current process controls for preventing or detecting failure modes.
13. Assign a detection level for each failure mode.
14. Calculate the risk priority number.
15. Specify recommended actions.
16. Assign actions to be taken and the responsible team member.
17. Recalculate the risk priority number.

(The steps above correspond to and are modified from those in *Potential Failure Mode and Effects Analysis (FMEA) Reference Manual*, developed by the Automotive Industry Action Group, Chrysler Corp., Ford Motor Co., and General Motors Corp. [1995, pp. 29–45].)

To understand this tool, it's better to view the entire form (Figure 5-6). Some of the terms are self-explanatory, but others are not:

#	Process Function (Step)	Potential Failure Modes (process defects) (Ys)	Potential Failure Effects (Ys)	S E V	Potential Causes of Failure (Xs)	O C C	Current Process Controls	D E T	R P N
1									
2									
3									

Figure 5-6. Sample FMEA table

- **Process Function (Step).** The description and purpose of each process step.
- **Potential Failure Modes.** The ways in which the process could fail to meet customer requirements—the actual defects.
- **Potential Failure Effects.** The possible effects of the failure mode on the customers.
- **SEV (Severity).** Rating (1–10), the seriousness of the failure mode.
- **Potential Causes of Failure.** How the failure could have occurred (X). Refers to the failure mode.
- **OCC (Occurrence).** Rating (1–10), the probability that the failure mode will occur.
- **DET (Detection).** Rating (1-10) is the ability to detect the failure mode.
- **RPN (Risk Priority Number).** A rating calculated by multiplying the three ratings: SEV x OCC x DET. The RPN is used to rank-order the concerns needing attention.

Here are some practical rules for using an FMEA:

- An RPN greater than 80 indicates a critical need requiring immediate action.
- A severity rating greater than 5 starts into safety-related defects.
- A high RPN with a low probability of detection—P(DET)—is likely to result in defects that escape internal tests and reach customers.
- A high probability of occurrence—P(OCC)—indicates poor capability.

Four charts (Figures 5-7 through 5-10) provide guidance for rating severity, occurrence, and detection.

Note: A caution must be highlighted here regarding the severity rating. You cannot ignore countermeasures with a standalone rating greater than or equal to 8. This is typically a safety issue that must be resolved immediately.

The Cpk in Figure 5-9 is the process capability index, a statistical measure of a process's ability to produce output within specification limits, used here as a measure for the probability of occurrence.

Because the FMEA isn't specifically intended to be an ongoing process documentation tool in the context of DMAIC, the team should use it on only a *part* of the process under consideration, not the entire

Effect	Criteria: Severity of Effect Defined	Ranking
Hazardous Without Warning	May endanger operator. Failure mode affects safe vehicle operation and/or involves noncompliance with government regulation. Failure will occur without warning.	10
Hazardous With Warning	May endanger operator. Failure mode affects safe vehicle operation and/or involves noncompliance with government regulation. Failure will occur with warning	9
Very High	Major disruption to production line. 100% of product may have to be scrapped. Vehicle/item inoperable, loss of primary function. Customers very dissatisfied.	8
High	Minor disruption to production line. A portion (less than 100%) of product may have to be scrapped. Vehicle/item operable, but at reduced level of performance. Customer dissatisfied.	7
Moderate	Minor disruption to production line. A portion (less than 100%) of product may have to be scrapped (no sorting). Vehicle/item operable, but some comfort/convenience items inoperable. Customers experience discomfort.	6
Low	Minor disruption to production line. 100% of product may have to be reworked. Vehicle/item operable, but some comfort/convenience items operable at reduced level of performance. Customers experience some dissatisfaction.	5
Very Low	Minor disruption to production line. The product may have to be resorted and a portion (less than 100%) may have to be reworked. Fit/finish/squeak/rattle item does not conform. Defect noticed by most customers.	4
Minor	Minor disruption to production line. A portion (less than 100%) of the product may have to be reworked online but out-of-station. Fit/finish/squeak/rattle item does not conform. Defect noticed by average customers.	3
Very Minor	Minor disruption to production line. A portion (less than 100%) of the product may have to be reworked online but out-of-station. Fit/finish/squeak/rattle item does not conform. Defect noticed by discriminating customers.	2
None	No effect.	1

Figure 5-7. Sample severity rating chart from the automotive industry (Source: AIAG, *Potential Failure Mode and Effects Analysis Reference Guide*, SAE J 1739, February 1993, p. 35.)

Effect	Criteria: Impact of Effect Defined	Ranking
Critical Business Unit-Wide	May endanger company ability to do business. Failure mode affects process operation and/or involve noncompliance with government regulation.	10
Critical Loss– Customer- Specific	May endanger relationship with customers. Failure mode affects product delivered and/or customer relationship due to process failure and/or noncompliance with government regulation.	9
High	Major disruption to process/production down situation. Results in near 100% rework or an inability to process. Customers very dissatisfied.	7
Moderate	Moderate disruption to process. Results in some rework or an inability to process. Process is operable, but some workarounds are required. Customers experience dissatisfaction.	5
Low	Minor disruption to process. Process can be completed with workarounds or rework at the back end. Results in reduced level of performance. Defect is noticed and commented upon by customers.	3
Minor	Minor disruption to process. Process can be completed with workarounds or rework at the back end. Results in reduced level of performance. Defect noticed internally but not externally.	2
None	No effect.	1

Figure 5-8. Sample severity rating chart for production (© Six Sigma Consultants, Inc.)

process. The part of the process to which the FMEA is applied is determined by the process map and the YX matrix. The part of the process with the highest-scoring X variables from the YX matrix is where the FMEA should be focused. In a perfect world, this might be a small part of the entire process. In reality, however, it is often several parts of the process that might not be adjacent. The black belt should use sound judgment in applying the FMEA, as it is necessary but time-consuming.

(The black belt might find that the FMEA will be an important part of the control plan in the Control phase. In that case it might actually become an ongoing documentation tool. In the Measure phase, however, FMEA should not be performed on the entire process, but only on the parts of the process of greatest interest, as indicated by the results of the YX matrix.)

Probability of Failure	Possible Failure Rates	Cpk	Ranking
Very High: Failure is almost inevitable	≥ 1 in 2	<0.33	10
	1 in 3	≥0.33	9
High: Generally associated with processes similar to previous processes that have often failed	1 in 8	≥0.51	8
	1 in 20	≥0.67	7
Moderate: Generally associated with processes that have experienced occasional failures but not in major proportions	1 in 80	≥0.83	6
	1 in 400	≥1.00	5
	1 in 2,000	≥1.17	4
Low: Isolated failures associated with similar processes	1 in 15,000	≥1.33	3
Very Low: Only isolated failures associated with almost identical processes	1 in 150,000	≥1.5	2
Remote: Failure unlikely. No failures ever associated with almost identical processes	1 in 1,500,000	≥1.67	1

Figure 5-9. Sample occurrence rating chart (Source: AIAG, *Potential Failure Mode and Effects Analysis Reference Guide*, SAE J 1739, February 1993, p. 39.)

Detection	**Criteria:** Likelihood the existence of a defect will be detected by the test method before product advances to next or subsequent processes	Ranking
Almost impossible	Test detects <80% of failures	10
Very remote	Test detects 80% of failures	9
Remote	Test detects 82.5% of failures	8
Very low	Test detects 85% of failures	7
Low	Test detects 87.5% of failures	6
Moderate	Test detects 90% of failures	5
Moderately high	Test detects 92.5% of failures	4
High	Test detects 95% of failures	3
Very high	Test detects 97.5% of failures	2
Almost certain	Test detects 99.5% of failures	1

Figure 5-10. Sample detection rating chart (Source: AIAG, *Potential Failure Mode and Effects Analysis Reference Guide*, SAE J 1739, February 1993, p. 41.)

Once the steps of the process to be documented with the FMEA are determined, list these steps in the Process Step column. Leave some space under each process step to allow for multiple-line entries related to the various failure modes and effects at each step. Keep in mind that each step can have several failure modes, each failure mode can have several causes, and each cause of a given failure mode can have a unique effect with different severities.

When we analyze the data collected during the Measure phase, it's important to understand how the failure modes affect critical-to-quality characteristics (the Ys). FMEA is a disciplined procedure that allows you to anticipate failures and prevent them. Identify ways the product or process can fail. Then plan to prevent those failures.

The FMEA and all the other tools used in the Measure phase are living documents. They must be updated and communicated to the people overseeing the process in question.

Step 4. Conduct a Measurement System Analysis (MSA)

Any time you measure the results of a process, you'll see some variation. This observed variation might result for either of two reasons. First, there are always variations in any process. Second, any method for taking measurements is imperfect; thus, there are always variations in any measurement system. The project team must determine whether any variation noted in the measurements is due to causes they need to identify and address or it's the effect of the measurement system.

If the variation is due to the process, the team will use statistical process control (SPC) to identify the sources and reduce that variation as much as possible. But before doing any SPC analyses, the team should determine to what extent the variation observed might be due to the measurement system.

Measurement system errors can be classified into two categories: accuracy and precision. *Accuracy* refers to the difference between recorded measurements and the actual values for the parts measured. *Precision* refers to the variation in measurements when a device is used to measure the same part repeatedly. Problems of either type can occur within any measurement system. For example, it's possible to have a device that measures parts very precisely (little variation in the measurements) but not accurately, or a device that is accurate (the average of the measurements is very close to the correct value), but not precise, i.e., there's a large variance in the measurements. It's also possible, of course, for a device to be neither accurate nor precise.

Imagine you're tossing a dozen darts at a dartboard. If they all end up clustered together away from the center, your tosses are precise but not accurate. If they end up scattered around the center, your tosses are accurate but not precise. If they end up scattered all over the board and maybe even on the wall, your tosses are neither precise nor accurate. If they end up crowded at the center, then your tosses are both precise and accurate.

These concepts of precision and accuracy are a little more complicated than in this simple example. As a champion, you should understand the basics, although you don't need to know as much as your black belts.

Accuracy

The concept of accuracy consists of three components: stability, bias, and linearity.

Stability is freedom from special-cause variation over time. A team can measure process stability with SPC, scatter plots, or other forms of statistical analysis.

Bias is the influence of any factor that causes the sample data to appear different from what it actually is. A team can measure process measurement bias by comparing the data average with a reference value.

Linearity is statistical consistency in measurements over the full range of expected values. A team can measure linearity using measurement standards calibrated to higher authorities, such as the National Institute of Standards and Technology.

Precision

The concept of precision consists of two components: reproducibility and repeatability.

Reproducibility is variation due to the measurement system. It's the variation observed when different operators measure different parts

Accuracy The difference between recorded measurements and the actual values for the parts measured. It consists of three components: stability, bias, and linearity.

KEY TERMS

Stability Freedom from special-cause variation over time.

Bias The influence of any factor that causes the sample data to appear different from what they actually are.

Linearity Statistical consistency in measurements over the full range of expected values.

Precision The variation in measurements when a device is used to measure the same part repeatedly. It consists of two components: reproducibility and repeatability.

Reproducibility Variation due to the measurement system. It's the variation observed when different operators measure different parts using the same device.

Repeatability Variation due to the measuring device. It's the variation observed when the same operator measures the same part with the same device repeatedly.

using the same device.

Repeatability is variation due to the measuring device, when the same operator measures the same part with the same device repeatedly.

Measurement Error

Measurement error could be reported as probable error, a reasonable estimate of typical uncertainty of any single measurement. *Probable error* defines the effective resolution of a given measurement. In essence, the probable error defines the confidence interval within which actual measurements exist. This becomes critical when making pass/fail decisions based on measurements.

Ideally, measurement system analysis (MSA) should take place at the outset of the Measure phase to ensure that the data used to track process performance and to reveal the nature of the defects are appropriately accurate, precise, and sensitive. As mentioned earlier, the reality of time constraints dictates that other project work—such as the sequence of process map, YX matrix, and FMEA—be initiated before the MSA is complete. In some cases, the MSA process can continue into the Analyze phase, but team members should understand that there is some risk in making bad decisions on bad data until the measurement system is assessed and improved.

The project team must collect measurement data on the CTQ characteristics. When there is variation in this data, it can be attributed either to the characteristic being measured or to the way measurements are being taken (measurement error). When there is a large measurement error, it affects the data and could lead to inaccurate decisions.

The primary contributors to measurement system error affect the spread of the distribution and describe the measuring system's precision—repeatability and reproducibility.

Since reproducibility and repeatability are important types of error, they are the object of a specific study called a *gauge (gage) repeatability and reproducibility study* (*gauge R&R*). This study can be performed on measurement systems whether based on attributes data or variables data.

Attributes data are data that fit into categories that can be described in terms of words (attributes)—such as good /bad, go/no-go, pass/fail,

---

Gauge (gage) repeatability and reproducibility study (gauge R&R) Statistical tool that measures the amount of variation in the measurement system arising from the measurement device and the people taking the measurement. A gauge R&R is not limited to gauges: It's used for all types of measuring instruments, test methods, and other measurement systems.

KEY TERM

---

correct/incorrect, yes/no—and counted.

An attribute study can be used on most transactional processes. For example, an invoice is filled out either correctly or incorrectly. It enables the evaluation of the consistency in measurements among operators, clerks, bookkeepers, or agents after having at least two people measure several parts or evaluate a transactional process step at random on a few trials. If there's no consistency, the measurement system must be improved.

Variables data are quantitative data. There are two types: Discrete data are counted, and continuous data are on a continuum, usually in decimal form.

Here are the basic steps for performing an MSA or a gauge R&R:

> **Attributes data** Data that fit into categories describable in terms of words (attributes)—such as good/bad, go/no-go, pass/fail, correct/incorrect, yes/no—and counted.
>
> **Variables data** Quantitative data consist of two types: Discrete data are counted, and continuous data are on a continuum, usually in decimal form.

KEY TERMS

1. Calibrate the measuring device or ensure that it's been calibrated.
2. Have each operator measure all the samples once in random order.
3. Repeat step 2 for the required number of trials.
4. Use a spreadsheet or software to determine the statistics of the R&R study (Figure 5-11).
5. Analyze the results and determine follow-up action, if any.

Figure 5-12 shows an example of a bad gauge R&R. This is Minitab

	Part 1	PART 1	PART 2	PART 3	PART 4	PART 5	PART 6	PART 7	PART 8	PART 9	PART 10
Operator 1	Measurement 1										
	Measurement 2										
Operator 2	Measurement 1		6 Measurements x 10 Parts								
	Measurement 2		That's 60 data points								
Operator 3	Measurement 1		3operators taking random								
	Measurement 2		measures of 10 different parts								

Figure 5-11. Layout of gauge R&R study

software output using a gauge run chart. (Minitab is the preferred analytical statistical software for Six Sigma.) You can use this chart to quickly assess the differences in measurements between or among different operators and parts. A stable process would give you a random horizontal scattering of points. With an operator or part effect, you would see some kind of pattern(s) in the plot.

Let's look at Part no. 3 and Operator 1, for example. The two black dots clearly show a large variation in that operator's measurements of this part.

Let's contrast those results with results from a good MSA or gauge R&R.

In this example, as shown in Figure 5-13, the three operators are con-

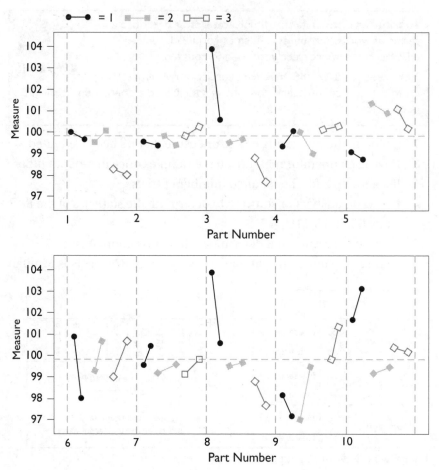

Figure 5-12. Example of a bad gauge R&R

sistent with each other in their measurements and none of the 10 parts is causing variation. This is how good your measurement system needs to work to ensure that the data you'll be analyzing are good. This is the goal to achieve!

Real Case Study: Rivets and Aircraft, Gauge R&R Study

Rivet height is a critical-to-quality characteristic in manufacturing aircraft. The rivets attach the skin of the aircraft to the frame and prevent them from separating in flight. Rivets that are not flush negatively affect the aerodynamics in terms of performance and fuel economy.

Bombardier Aerospace had a problem with the rivets it was using to

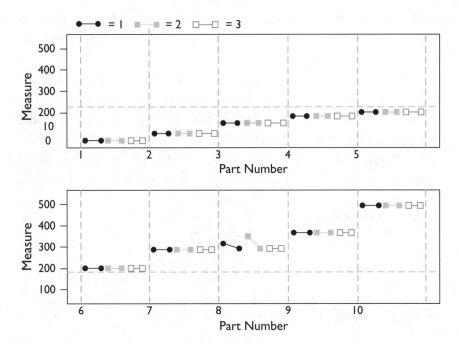

Figure 5-13. Example of a good gauge R&R

assemble aircraft. The rivets supplied had a high defect rate. They called us in to help solve the problem.

The black belt decided to do an attribute gauge study of an assembly process using an Excel spreadsheet. Here's how he described the procedure to the team members. I select 20 rivets that have been installed on my sample parts. Referring to the specifications of these parts, I know which ones have been installed slightly below or above limits. I take note of the rivets that are good and bad and enter them into my data spreadsheet, in the Attribute column. This will enable me to determine how consistently operators evaluate a set of samples against a known standard, which we refer to as Attribute."

A team member asked, "But how do you evaluate the consistency between them?"

The black belt explained: "Well, I'm going to work with both the day and night shift machine operators. They'll both measure the 20 rivets of this sample twice, which are provided to them in a random order. Meanwhile, I'll record all their measurements for both trials in my spreadsheet so that we can compare these scores with the standard scores that I've already entered. This will provide us with the data necessary to evaluate the measurement system."

After the operators took their measurements and the black belt recorded the data, he presented the results to his team (Figure 5-14).

The Appraiser Score shows how consistently the operators were able to repeat their own measurements. This score was obtained by comparing each operator's trials for all samples to determine the proportion of consistent scores. The Score vs. Attribute value showed how consistent

Attribute Legend
G =   Good
NG = Not Good

Scoring Report
Date   8-15-2014
Name   Dep. 282 Boeing
Product Rivets
SBU 148T2610-238
Test Conditions GT996645-GTOO01 (Mod)

Known Population		Operator #1		Operator #2		Y/N	Y/N
Sample #	Attribute	Try #1	Try #2	Try #1	Try #2	Agree	Agree
1	G	G	G	G	G	Y	Y
2	G	G	G	G	G	Y	Y
3	G	G	G	G	G	Y	Y
4	G	G	G	G	G	Y	Y
5	G	G	G	G	G	Y	Y
6	G	NG	G	G	G	N	N
7	G	G	G	G	G	Y	Y
8	G	G	G	G	G	Y	Y
9	NG	G	G	NG	NG	N	N
10	NG	NG	NG	G	G	N	N
11	G	G	G	G	G	Y	Y
12	G	G	G	G	G	Y	Y
13	NG	NG	NG	NG	NG	Y	Y
14	G	G	G	G	G	Y	Y
15	G	G	G	G	G	Y	Y
16	G	G	G	G	G	Y	Y
17	NG	NG	NG	NG	NG	Y	Y
18	G	G	G	G	G	Y	Y
19	G	G	G	G	G	Y	Y
20	G	G	G	G	G	Y	Y
	% Appraiser Score	95.00%		100.00%			
	% Scope vs. Attribute	90.00%		95.00%			
				Screen% Effective Score		85.00%	
				Screen% Effective Score vs. Attribute			85.00%

Figure 5-14. Gauge R&R attribute study

the operators' measurements were with the known standard, in the Attribute column.

Here, we take the attributes from trials 1 and 2 and calculate the proportion of scores that are consistent across the samples. The results for operator 1 are 95% (19/20) between the two trials and 90% (18/20) for the Score vs. Attribute value. For operator 2, the appraiser score was 100% and the Score vs. Attribute was 95%.

We also want to know how consistent our measurement decisions are overall. In this case, we want to know the effective scores for both operators. Then we want to compare the effective score with the standard score. The target value is 100%, meaning that all measurement decisions are consistent.

In our case, both scores are 85%. We obtain these numbers by comparing all of both operators' scores for both trials for all 20 samples and determining the proportion of consistent samples. When measurement decisions are inconsistent, it means we should improve our measurement system by improving the measuring method and/or the measurement device or by providing better operator training.

The black belt also does an attribute agreement analysis in Minitab. The analysis includes confidence intervals around the appraiser.

An attribute agreement analysis evaluates the impact of repeatability and reproducibility on accuracy, that is, it evaluates the ability of each person who is appraising attribute data to get the same results on several occasions (repeatability), the same results as people appraising the same data (reproducibility), and the same results as an expert or results that are correct (overall accuracy).

Minitab displays three assessment agreement tables: Each Appraiser vs. Standard, Between Appraisers, and All Appraisers vs. Standard. Each percentage of matches is associated with a *confidence interval* (CI), an estimate of the probability that the true population mean lies within a range around a sample mean. (We don't get into those specifics here.)

The concept of the MSA is critical to the DMAIC problem-solving process because we need to trust the data we get through our measurements. If there's a problem with our measurement system and we assume it's OK, then the rest of the work we do will be one big defect.

Step 5. Determine Process Capability

A process is capable to the extent that it's stable and the output values are within the upper and lower specification limits, that is, the output meets customer requirements.

But what is "stable"? Process stability is one of the most important concepts of Six Sigma. Unfortunately, practitioners don't agree on a single definition of stability. In theory, no process is truly stable. In practical terms, a process can be considered stable if only chance variation exists. If a process shows any systematic variation beyond a certain degree, then it's considered unstable. However you define stability, the less stable the process, the more problematic any attempt to assess its capability.

The specification limits define the range of acceptable deviation from the target value. In simple terms, *process capability* is the ability of a process to meet the specifications for a product or service; it's a statistical measure of inherent variability for a given characteristic. The less variation, the better.

> **KEY TERM**
> **Process capability** Ability of a process to meet the specifications of a product or service; a statistical measure of inherent variability for a given characteristic.

Process variability can be measured in two ways: at a specified time and over time. What matters is not that a process can meet specifications at one point in time, but rather, how it performs over time. Of course, short-term performance is less important than long-term performance. The project team assesses process capability to determine whether a process, given its natural short-term variation, has the potential long-term capability to meet established customer requirements or specifications.

What's the difference between short-term capability and long-term capability?

A short-term capability study covers a relatively short period (days or weeks) and consists of 30–50 data points. It measures the *potential* capability of the process, what the process should be able to achieve.

A long-term capability study covers a relatively long period (weeks or months) and consists of 100–200 data points. It measures the *actual* capability of the process.

Standard Deviation

Standard deviation, mentioned briefly in Chapter 1, is a measure of the amount of variation from the mean in a distribution of values of a characteristic. It's calculated as the square root of the variance, which is the average of the squared differences from the mean.

There are programs that calculate standard deviation. This calculation consists of three steps:

KEY TERMS

Standard deviation A measure of the amount of variation from the mean in a distribution of values of a characteristic, calculated as the square root of the variance, which is the average of the squared differences from the mean.

Variance Average of the Squared Differences from the Mean Subtract each value from the mean, square the difference, then find the average of those squared differences.

1. Find the mean, the average of all the values collected. Total those values and divide the sum by the number of values.
2. Find the variance, the average of the squared differences from the mean. In other words, for each value, subtract the mean and square the difference. (The differences are both plus and minus numbers, which would add up to 0 and get us nowhere. Squaring converts negative differences to positive.) Then find the average of those squared differences.
3. Find the square root of the variance.

Process Capability Indices

There are four commonly used measures of process capability—Cp, Cpk, Pp, and Ppk. Cpk and Ppk are sometimes called process *performance* indices, to distinguish them from Cp and Pp, process *capability* indices. Cp and Cpk are used for *short-term* capability, while Pp and Ppk are used for *long-term* capability.

Cp indicates the short-term level of performance that a process can potentially achieve. It does not consider the center of the process; it estimates the "instantaneous capability" of the process. Cp is the tolerance width (distance between the specification limits) divided by the short-term spread of the process (six times the short-term standard deviation).

BEWARE OR BE BEWILDERED

CAUTION Cp is generally a short-term index, and Pp is generally a long-term index. However, sometimes people use Pp for short term and Cp for long term. Use of any of these capability indices should include wording to specify what's meant.

$$Cp = (USL) - (LSL) / 6\sigma \text{ ST}$$

Cp expresses the relationship between the width of the spread and the tolerance width. The calculation does not consider the specification limits.

When we calculate the Cp, what do the results mean? The higher the Cp value, the better the process. Cp = 2 represents the short-term objective for process capability.

Cp Process capability index, calculated as the tolerance width divided by the short-term process spread.

KEY TERMS **Tolerance width** Distance between the upper specification limit and the lower specification limit.

Process spread Extent to which values for a process characteristic vary, often shown as the process average plus and minus a number of standard deviations. Short-term process spread represents six times the short-term standard deviation, that is, ±3σ ST.

- If *Cp* < 1, the process output exceeds specifications. The process is incapable.
- If *Cp* = 1, the process barely meets specifications. There is a probability that at least 0.3% defects will be produced—and even more if the process is not centered.
- If *Cp* > 1, the process output falls within specifications but defects might be produced if the process is not centered on the target value.

Cp is used for continuous data and is based on two assumptions: that the process is statistically stable and that the data are approximately normally distributed (i.e., forming a bell-shaped curve on a histogram).

Because *Cp* does not consider the specification limits (process centering), it should not be used alone to describe process performance. If the process mean is not centered, Cp overestimates process capability. Use Cp in conjunction with Cpk, which considers process centering.

Cpk is a measure of the capability of a process to meet established customer requirements or specifications, given its short-term variation. It assumes that process output is distributed approximately normally.

> **Cpk** A measure of the capability of a process to meet established customer requirements or specifications, given its short-term variation. It's the lesser of two values—the Cpu (difference between USL and mean, divided by three times the short-term standard deviation) and the Cpl (difference between LSL and mean, divided by three times the short-term standard deviation).
>
> **KEY TERM**

Cpk is the lesser of two values—the Cpu and the Cpl. The *Cpu* is the difference between the upper specification limit (USL) and the mean, divided by three times the short-term standard deviation. The *Cpl* is the difference between the lower specification limit (LSL) and the mean, divided by three times the short-term standard deviation.

$$Cpu = (USL - mean) / 3\sigma \; ST$$
$$Cpl = (LSL - mean) / 3\sigma \; ST$$

Cpk indicates the level of performance that a process can achieve, taking into account the location of the process mean. When the process is centered, $Cpu = Cpl = Cpk = Cp$.

When we calculate the Cpk, what do the results mean? We want a Cpk of at least 1.33.

- If $Cpk = Cp$, the process mean is on target.
- If $Cpk = 0$, the process mean falls on one of the specification limits: 50% of the process output is beyond the specification limits.
- If $Cpk < -1$, the process mean is completely outside the specification limits: 100% of the process output is beyond the specification limits.

Cpk is used for continuous data and is based on two assumptions: that the process is statistically stable and that its data are approximately normally distributed. However, Cpk should not be used alone to describe process capability. It should be used in conjunction with Cp, the short-term process capability index.

Once you understand the process capability indices Cp and Cpk, it's relatively easy to understand the performance indices Pp and Ppk. These are long-term measures.

If the data distribution is not normal, don't panic. Nonnormality is a way of life, because no characteristic (height, weight, etc.) will produce an exactly normal distribution.

However, most technical statistical gurus will drive you to transform the data. Transformation is one strategy for making nonnormal data resemble normal data.

Why is normal or "normalized" data better? The most important reason is because many statistical models are based on the mean and on the assumption that the mean is an appropriate measure of central tendency, that is, the center or middle of a distribution. There are other measures of central tendency, including two with which you're familiar—the median and the mode, but the mean is generally a better measure.

SMART
MANAGING

USING STATISTICAL TOOLS

The *median* of a set of data values is the midpoint.
The *mode* of a set of data values is the value that occurs most often.

There are disadvantages to using the mean as a measure of central tendency, notably that it becomes less reliable when extreme values exist. For example, consider this series of values: 1, 20, 23, 18, 23. The mean would be 17, which is lower than four of the five values. Both the mode, 23, and the median, 20, would be better measures of the central tendency as they are generally less affected by extreme values, outliers.

Data transformation is the application of a mathematical modification to the values of a variable. There are various possible data transformations; the transformations most commonly used to improve the normality of variables are square root, log, and inverse. These transformations affect the nature of the variables, making interpretation of the results more complex.

Nonnormal data are OK. You can transform the data, but the bottom line is that when a process that's repetitive in producing many (> 100) parts or transactions per hour, you should be asking questions. Why is the data for this process not normal? What's causing the nonnormality? Is it caused by different people, different shifts, materials, adjustments, or techniques? What are the factors? Those are the problems to solve.

You could transform the data to look more normal, but the problem still exists. Contrary to mathematical theory, it's incorrect to use a "normal analysis" tool on nonnormal data. True! However, what matters is capability in terms of the specs. Let's consider an example.

Real Case Study: Rivets and Aircraft, Process Capability

Let's return to our case of the problem with rivet height at Bombardier Aerospace.

As mentioned earlier, we first did a gauge study of the measurement system to ensure that the data we used were valid. Next, we collected data, using a rational data collection plan. The logical sampling needed to cover five kinds of variation: batch-to-batch variation, shift-to-shift variation, operator-to-operator variation, tool-to-tool variation, and variation over different products over time.

Figure 5-15 shows the distribution of rivets we sampled for height at Bombardier, with the LSL at 4 mm and the USL at 5 mm. (The data presented are coded to protect product confidentiality.)

Let's look at two capability indices here, Cp and Pp. Cp is the process capability index. Pp is the process performance index—overall capability—which verifies whether a specific sample is capable of meeting customer CTQs. Process performance differs from process capability in that process performance applies only to a specific sample.

Pp, overall capability, is 0.39, which translates to a sigma value of 1.17. Cp, potential within-part variation, is 1.42, which translates to a sigma value of 4.26. The graphic clearly shows why we should not trust the numbers alone. Here the Cp would cause us to come to the wrong conclusion. You must always look at both the long term and the short term for the whole picture.

This graph shows that this data set is nonnormal. From the two curves we know that the distribution is bimodal.

Contrast this Bombardier data with the Boeing data for rivet height (Figure 5-16).

First, look at the specification limits for Boeing: LSL = 4.3 mm; USL = 4.7 mm. The spread between the spec limits is less than for Bombardier, with its LSL at 4.0 mm and USL at 5.0 mm.

Next, look at the distribution: Their data are normal and the tools work!

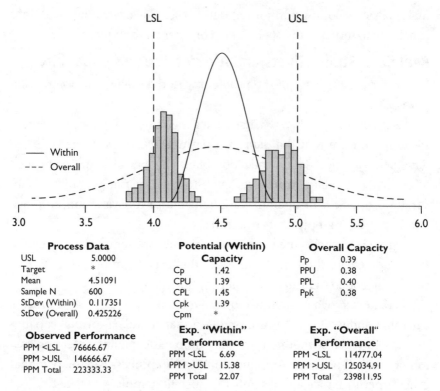

Figure 5-15. Rivet height, Bombardier

Can you figure out why the Bombardier distribution for rivets from the same supplier is bimodal, not normal like the Boeing distribution?

This is a classic supplier quality problem! The supplier is sorting through the rivets it produces and sending the good rivets to Boeing and the leftovers to Bombardier. Distributions like this really happen. If you were to transform the data, as some gurus would advise, you would miss the problem.

Be careful about these gurus—and be sure to focus on the problem, not the manipulation of data!

Z Scores and Sigma Shift

This discussion of capability would not be complete if we didn't discuss Z scores and the sigma shift.

A *Z score* (aka *sigma score* or *standard score*) is a measure of the dis-

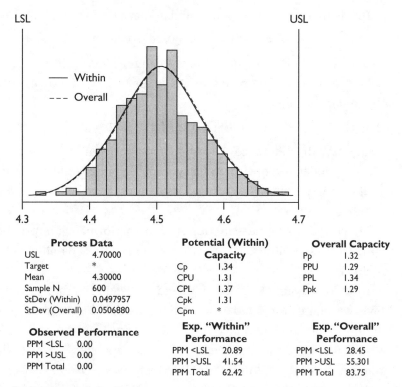

Figure 5-16. Rivet height, Boeing

tance between a sample value from a data set and the mean for that data set, expressed in terms of standard deviations. The Z score allows us to calculate the probability of a value occurring within a normal distribution and to compare values from different normal distributions. A low Z score means a significant amount of data distribution extends past the specification limit. A higher Z score means the process is producing fewer defects.

> **Z score** (aka **sigma score** or **standard score**) Measure of the distance between a sample value from a data set and the mean for that data set, expressed in terms of standard deviations. **KEY TERM**

To find the Z score of a sample value, do the following:

1. Find the mean and the standard deviation for the set of data.
2. Find the difference between the sample value and the mean.

3. Divide that difference by the standard deviation.

Z = x – mean / standard deviation

Here our calculations get a little more interesting.

We've discussed the Cp and the Pp. These two indices are calculated with the same formula:

USL – LSL / 6σ

So, what's the difference? The calculation of sigma.

The Cp index is a measure of a system's potential ability to produce output within spec limits. It's a measure of short-term capability and uses an estimated sigma.

The Pp index is a measure of a system's performance in producing output within spec limits. It's a measure of long-term capability and uses actual sigma.

If you look again at Figures 5-15 and 5-16, you see that each graph shows two figures for standard deviation, one labeled "Within" (corresponding to the Cp, "Potential [Within] Capability") and the other labeled "Overall" (corresponding to the Pp, "Overall Capability"). So, for Bombardier we have StDev(Within) = 0.117351 and StDev(Overall) = 0.425226. For Boeing we have StDev(Within) = 0.0497957 and StDev(Overall) = 0.0506880.

Since Z is calculated using sigma, guess what! Yes, Z has a split personality because of the two ways of calculating sigma: We have Z_{st} for short-term capability when special factors are removed and the process is centered properly, and Z_{lt} for long-term capability.

The short-term Z score, Z_{st}, represents the best performance to be expected from the process. It's an idealistic capability measure based on a relatively small sample of measurements from the process. Over time, however, a process tends not to operate up to its potential.

So the Six Sigma pioneers developed a method for using short-term idealistic capability to project realistic, long-term performance. They shifted the short-term process distribution closer to the specification limits by 1.5 times the short-term standard deviation so as to approximate the performance of the process in the long term.

Thus we measure the short-term capability of a process and we calcu-

WHY 1.5 SIGMA? SMART

Processes vary over time. The Six Sigma pioneers at Motorola decided the typical variation was between 1.4 and 1.6 sigma. They called this the Long-Term Dynamic Mean Variation.

MANAGING

Mikel J. Harry and Richard Schroeder, Motorola employees who founded the Six Sigma Academy and wrote *Six Sigma, The Breakthrough Management Strategy Revolutionizing the World's Top Corporations*, called this 1.5 sigma shift their "fudge factor."

late its short-term Z score. Then we use the short-term Z score with a 1.5 short-term standard deviation shift to calculate the expected long-term Z score.

The simple formula is $Z_{st} = Cp_3$. For example, if Cp = 1, then Z_{st} = 3 sigma, and if Cp = 2, then $Z_{st} = 6\sigma$.

Measure Phase-Gate Review

As mentioned in Chapter 3, each of the five DMAIC phases ends with a review to determine whether the project team has performed the activities specified for that phase in the project plan and achieved the stated objectives. At the end of the Measure phase, the black belt reports to the executive team on the project's status. The review gives the executive team an opportunity to ask questions about the project, make comments, discuss obstacles, allocate resources as necessary, ensure that the project team is achieving the project goals according to schedule, and provide positive reinforcement to the project team. The reviews can be both technical and nontechnical.

The review for the Measure phase varies according to the project specifics because there's no set sequence of steps that every team must follow and no tools that every team must use. Teams must use logic and their knowledge of the situation to determine which steps to follow and select appropriate tools.

Manager's Checklist for Chapter 5

☑ The Measure phase is the start of the DMAIC problem-solving process.

☑ The critical tools of the Measure phase are process mapping, YX matrix, failure modes and effects analysis (FMEA), measurement system analysis (MSA), and process capability analysis.

☑ In mapping a process map, there are two critical questions:
1. Why do we do this step?
2. How do we know the result is good?

☑ The simple equation for six sigma is $Z_{st} = Cp * 3$. You achieve six sigma quality when you can have the entire 1.5σ shift and the $Cp = 2.0$ and the $Cpk = 1.5$.

Analyze Phase

We can't solve problems by using the same kind of thinking we used when we created them.

—Albert Einstein (1879-1955)

The purposes of the Analyze phase are to (1) evaluate and reduce the variables using graphical analysis and hypothesis testing and (2) identify the vital few factors in order to identify the root cause(s) of the defects. The team members examine the processes that affect the CTQs, and the black belt uses statistical tools to decide which Xs are the vital few that must be controlled to result in the desired improvement in the Ys.

The Analyze phase helps to quantify the performance gap and the benefits of improving the process and to generate ideas for improvement. In some cases during the Analyze phase, one factor might prove to be the largest contributor to the defect levels. Once the factor has proven the hypothesis and the defect rate can be switched on and off, the project is complete and there's no need to go through the Improve and Control phases.

In simple terms, the purpose of the Analyze phase is to sort through all the potential Xs that are causing the costly defects. It's like pouring all the Xs through a funnel so that the resulting output is the vital few Xs that are causing the defects.

In the Analyze phase, we start to break the problem into its vital few fac-

---

LUMPS IN THE EXTRUSION?

A plant in Batesville, Arkansas makes vehicle sealant for the automotive industry. The biggest problem, they believed, was "lumps in the extrusion" of rubber that was being used as the sealant. After basic analysis using simple tools such as Pareto charts and comparing other defect types, we discovered that "lumps in the extrusion" was not the biggest problem. It was 6th in terms of defect level and 10th in terms of cost. When the facts showed the actual causes of the problem, the company was able to work at solving more important problems and saving more money than if it had focused on "lumps in the extrusion"—one of the "trivial many" factors.

---

tors. We draw and sort through all the factors we started to list in the Measure phase. The list typically grows during the Analyze phase because we are starting to ask different questions. The last thing your company needs is to fix a political or mythical problem that results in no financial gain!

The Analyze phase is the portion of the project where the black belt works closely with the project team to review the collected data and to form hypotheses that the team will test. We discuss hypothesis testing later in this chapter, but we briefly mention it here.

A hypothesis, in its simple form, is a question. For example, if I change a setting from level A to level B, will the defect go away? Or if this person does the service rather than that person, will there be a difference in the service call rates? We are basically making comparisons.

You're going to prove or disprove the question you state in your hypothesis, but you'll state the risk of being right in terms of a percent of confidence. Typically in Six Sigma, we would aim at a 95% confidence in our answer. This is the phase where many of the trivial Xs are eliminated and the vital few Xs are analyzed more closely. The goal is to extract the vital few factors to prepare for the Improve phase, which is discussed in the next chapter.

Analyze Phase Activities

Figure 6-1 shows the typical activities of the Analyze phase.

You will have already completed an initial list of Xs during the Measure phase, some with data and some with simply a basic hypothesis that you want to test for significance. It's important to keep track of the Xs by

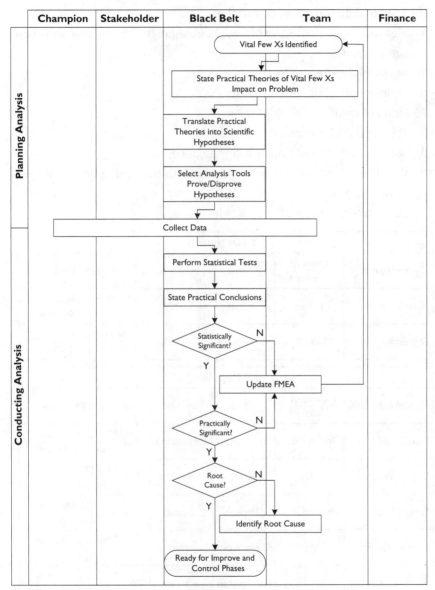

Figure 6-1. Analyze phase: Flow diagram

using a list or a tool that I recommend called an X Tracker™ (Shainin LLC). A sample format is shown in Figure 6-2. There are 11 items to track:

1. Name of the output (Y);
2. Units of measure (UOM) for Y;

3. Type of data (attribute or variable);
4. Measurement system analysis (MSA) (gauge R&R)—how well you can measure;
5. Name of the data collection file;
6. Description of the input factors (Xs);
7. Units of measure (UOM) for Xs;
8. Type of data (attribute or variable);
9. Statistical tool used to prove significance;
10. Vital (yes or no)—whether the Xs are of statistical significance for the Ys or not; and
11. Data collection files of the Xs being tested.

Y (Outputs)				
Description of Y	Units of Measure	Type	MSA Results	File Name
Hole Location	Inches	Variable	10%	My Documents\ HoleLocGR&R.mtw
Deburring	Good/Bad	Attribute	90%	My Documents\ DeburAttrGR&R.mtw

X (Inputs)					
Description of X	Units of Measure	Type	Tool Used	Vital	File Name
Line Speed	Inches/min	Continuous	Regression	Yes	My Documents\ LineSpeed.mtw
Day of Week	Day	Discrete	Box Plot	No	My Documents\ Day.mtw
Setup Method	Method A, B	Discrete	T-test	Yes	My Documents\ Method.mtw
Tumble Speed	RPM	Continuous	Scatter Plot	Yes	My Documents\ Speed.mtw
Abrasive Age	Hours	Continuous	Box Plot	No	My Documents\ AbrasiveAge.mtw

Figure 6-2. The X-Tracker™ used to track the Xs

In the Analyze phase, the project team may encounter two problems: (1) team members may not participate enough and (2) data for making decisions and monitoring the process may be inadequate.

If the data that exist for the process are inadequate, the problem probably has no quick cure. Black belts should be prepared to spend time either researching old records or collecting new information on the process that reflects the reality of the defect. In some cases the team may have to install a data collection process. This can be tedious and time-consuming, but crucial to ensure a successful Six Sigma project. Without valid data the team will not progress! It may be necessary to enlist the champion to make the needed resources available.

Whatever the situation, the black belt should ensure that the data collected has a purpose, that the team isn't collecting data simply to collect it or to satisfy an undefined insecurity or a nonvalue-added political purpose.

WORKING WITH WARPING

Here's a true story. The AlliedSignal Automotive plant in Clearfield, Utah, was producing an oil filter end cap with a whopping 200,000 defective parts per million. One of the hypotheses was that the shape of the end cap was warping. The hypothesis test proved there was a statistical and practical difference in the defect rate when the end cap warping was below a certain dimension. Basically, you either had a warp or you didn't. The defect rate dropped to 100 parts per million.

The black belt in this case fixed the problem in the Analyze phase and went on to a second project. This is a typical finding that you can dramatically reduce or even eliminate the defect in the Analyze phase. However, you still always need to control the Xs you found that are causing the defect.

In the case of the end cap described in the sidebar, testing the hypothesis proved there was a difference of statistical and practical significance in the defect rate when the warping was below a certain dimension. Statistical significance is calculated as the probability that an observed effect is occurring by chance. It's a statement of confidence or a risk of a difference detected in a sample of data not found in another data sample. For example, one might state there's a 95% confidence that if an end cap warped above a certain dimension it would be defective, with a 5% chance of being wrong. Practical significance relates the difference to a business or financial benefit. In our example, the practical difference is that reducing the warping to below that certain dimension reduced the

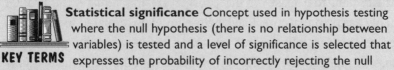

KEY TERMS

Statistical significance Concept used in hypothesis testing where the null hypothesis (there is no relationship between variables) is tested and a level of significance is selected that expresses the probability of incorrectly rejecting the null hypothesis. Statistical significance is mathematical: It derives from your data (sample size) and from your confidence (how confident you want to be in your results).

Practical significance Difference that will affect a decision. Practical significance is more subjective than statistical significance. Practical significance is based on factors such as cost, requirements, and objectives or targets.

defect rate from 200,000 ppm to 100 ppm. A difference can be of practical but not statistical significance and, conversely, a difference can be of statistical but not practical significance.

Analyze Phase Tools

Let's look at the basic tools used in the Analyze phase. We review some graphical tools with examples to help us set up statistical hypotheses. By representing the data graphically, we can look for critical Xs. Graphical analysis or data demographics show where the opportunities are for determining which Xs affect the desired Ys. Data demographics in this context is the study of the data population and its vital factors.

Make a mental note that you're typically looking for sources of variation within a process or product, between processes or products, and over time.

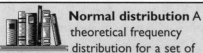

KEY TERM

Normal distribution A theoretical frequency distribution for a set of variable data that's symmetrical around the mean, usually represented by a bell-shaped curve. In the ideal normal distribution, the mean, median, and mode are equal.

An important concept in graphical analysis is *normality*, which is when data values are plotted and the distribution is symmetrical around the mean, tailing off symmetrically away from the mean.

In reality, data aren't often distributed normally. The challenge for the black belt and the project team is to break down the vital factors that cause a distribution to be nonnormal. Typically, when the display of data does not show a normal distribution, it's a major indicator that there are distributions within the overall data set that are normal, but are not aligned with the desired output. Such distributions can reveal clues for sources of variation. We should be happy when the data distributions aren't normal, because nonnormality suggests ways to search for sources of variation (Xs).

Figure 6-3 outlines guidelines for the Analyze phase. It includes the basic tools typically used in this phase.

Scope	Activities	Tools
Define performance objectives.	Develop analysis plan. Do graphical data analysis.	Histogram Box plots Dot plots Multivari analysis
Document potential Xs.	Identify root causes. Perform statistical tests.	Cause-and-effect (fishbone) diagram Interval plots Scatter plots Time series plots Hypothesis tests (Minitab)
Analyze source of variability.	Identify potential factors.	Multivari analysis Hypothesis tests (Minitab) ANOVA Regression

Figure 6-3. Analyze phase guidelines

These are the basic tools used in the Analyze phase:

- Histograms
- Box plots
- Dot plots
- Multivari analysis
- Cause-and-effect diagrams
- Interval plots
- Time series plots
- Scatter plots
- Regression
- Hypothesis testing
- Analysis of variance (ANOVA)

Data demographics come from Measure phase tools, namely the

process map, YX diagram, FMEA, and cause-and-effect (fishbone) diagram. Additional places to gather data should be other data collection sources such as databases, check sheets, and audits. Focus on the top Xs from the YX diagram. Variability in Ys happens for a reason. Data demographics are other process characteristics (potential Xs) that may have changed when Y is changed. Here are some examples of data demographics:

- **Time.** Shift, hourly events, time series of an event, day of the week, week of the month, season of the year.
- **Location/position.** Facility, region, branch, division, office, pod, cell, unit, machine, within a piece, between pieces.
- **Operator/clerk.** Training, experience, skill, technique, name, method, SOP used.

What are the data demographics in your area?

Histograms

A *histogram*, or *frequency plot chart*, is a bar graph that displays the relative frequency of continuous data values. The data values are sorted into incremental bins. For example, if machine bolts are being measured, the lengths might be grouped in increments of 1 millimeter: 10–11, 11–12, 12–13, and so on. The widths of the bars are proportional to the increments for the continuous data values (bins), and the heights of the bars are proportional to the frequencies (counts), showing the shape, centering, and spread of the data distribution.

Figure 6-4 shows a histogram that displays the lengths of 50 machine bolts.

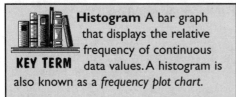

KEY TERM **Histogram** A bar graph that displays the relative frequency of continuous data values. A histogram is also known as a *frequency plot chart*.

Box Plots

Figure 6-5 shows a *box plot*, or *box-and-whisker plot*, which is a basic graphing tool that displays five points representing the centering, spread, and distribution of a set of continuous data. The plot consists of a box, whiskers, and outliers, and shows the maximum value, minimum value, median, 75th percentile (third quartile), and 25th percentile (first quartile).

This may sound complicated, but it's a handy way to show five points of information in one graphic. A box is drawn (vertically or horizontally) so

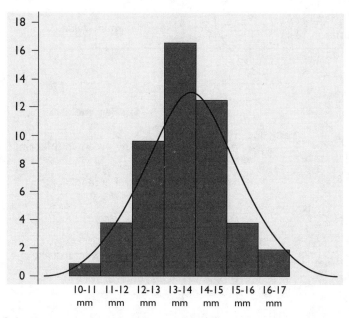

Figure 6-4. Histogram, lengths of machine bolts

that one end indicates the third quartile (Q3, or 75th percentile) and the other end indicates the first quartile (Q1, or 25th percentile). Typically, a line across the box shows the median of the distribution (second quartile, Q2, or 50th percentile). From each end of the box a line is drawn (a whisker); the lines extend to

> **Box Plot**
>
> A graph that displays five points representing the centering, spread, and distribution of a set of continuous data. **TOOLS** The plot consists of a box, whiskers, and outliers, and shows the maximum value, minimum value, median, 75th percentile (third quartile), and 25th percentile (first quartile). Also known as a *box-and-whisker plot*.

the maximum and minimum values. Outliers—points outside the upper and lower limits—are plotted with dots and sometime asterisks. Figure 6-5 illustrates how a box plot shows the five points of information for the data represented by the distribution curve.

Here's a real-life example of box plots. A company with two customer service call centers was studying the potential Xs that influenced performance (call times in seconds—faster is better). The Xs here were loca-

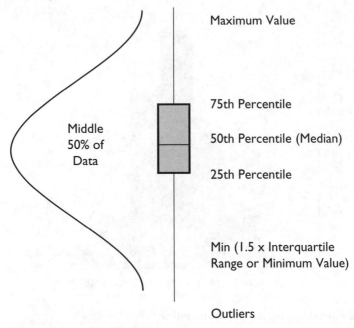

Maximum Value

75th Percentile

50th Percentile (Median)

25th Percentile

Middle
50% of
Data

Min (1.5 x Interquartile
Range or Minimum Value)

Outliers

Figure 6-5. Box plot with distribution curve

tion (Georgia and Nevada), method (expert and team), and time of day
(10 a.m., 1 p.m., and 5 p.m.). Figure 6-6 shows how we used box plots to
display data for each of those three Xs.

The power of the box plot is in showing the entire data set, multiple
distributions, on a single graph.

Dot Plots

Figure 6-7 shows a *dot plot*, a simple graphical display of data points of a
noncontinuous variable, with each observation represented by a dot
placed above a horizontal line marked with a range of values. The display
is similar to a histogram (with a horizontal axis), but the axis is divided
into more classes; ideally,
each distinct observation
would have its own plotting
position.

The dot plot is an excel-
lent tool to ensure that the box
plot confirms a conclusion or

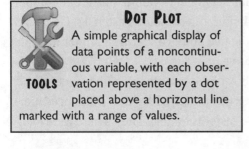

DOT PLOT
A simple graphical display of
data points of a noncontinuous variable, with each obser-
TOOLS   vation represented by a dot
placed above a horizontal line
marked with a range of values.

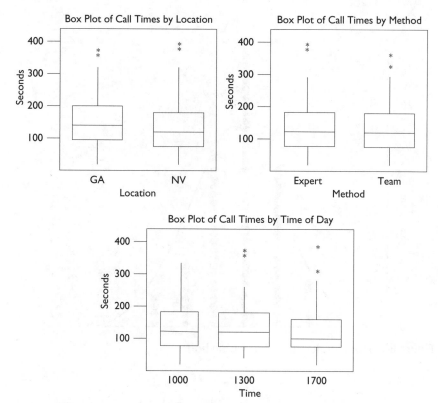

Figure 6-6. Box plots, call times by location, method, and time of day

a basic check by ensuring that outlier or specific individual data points don't skew the conclusion and lead to the wrong decision.

Look at the box plot in Figure 6-8. From the quartiles and the maximum and minimum values, we assume that the distribution of values is normal.

However, we'd be wrong, as we realize when we make a dot plot of the data (Figure 6-9). The dot plot clearly shows two data distributions, with one concentration of dots in the 10s and another in the 50s.

This is called a bimodal distribution: The data set has two most frequent values, which are evident in the dot plot, but not in the box plot. We can use a dot plot as a check for the box plot.

> **Bimodal** Data distribution for a data set with two most frequent values, resulting in two distinct distributions.
>
> **KEY TERM**

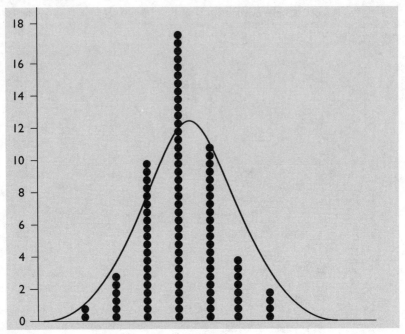

Figure 6-7. Dot plot, lengths of machine bolts

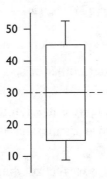

Figure 6-8. Box plot, simple example

Suppose we measure the length of the bolts we're producing. If we display the results with a box plot, the data may seem to be distributed normally, judging from the quartiles and maximum and minimum values. But when we display the results with a dot plot, we may discover the data distribution is actually bimodal. In this case, the bolts are coming from two machines. We measured the bolts as if they were a single popu-

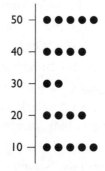

Figure 6-9. Dot plot, simple example

lation, as if the two machines were producing identical bolts, when we should have treated them as two populations.

It's always a good idea to perform checks and balances on data sets by looking at individual data as well as the overall total distribution. Dot plots are especially useful for comparing distributions. We could also do a check by using a histogram.

Multivari Analysis

Multivari analysis is a graphical analysis technique used to identify and quantify dominant sources of variation in a process when the Ys are continuous and the Xs are discrete. Multivari analysis is a passive study: Data are gathered and plotted with the objective of finding the largest source of variation. Multivari

>
> **MULTIVARI ANALYSIS**
> A technique used to identify and quantify dominant sources of variation in a process when the Ys are continuous and the Xs are discrete.
> **TOOLS**

> **Continuous (data)** Characteristic of numerical data that can only be counted, for example, the number of people in a department, nails produced in an hour. **KEY TERMS**
> **Discrete (data)** Characteristic of numerical data that can be measured, for example, heights of people in a department, length of nails, weight of bolts, temperature of oven, humidity.

analysis is not a means of experimenting with the process. The process is monitored in its natural, unchanged state.

To evaluate the effects of inputs on outputs, you create a multivari chart. A multivari chart shows how Xs can affect a Y by displaying patterns of variation within a subgroup of data, between subgroups of data, or data over time. A multivari chart enables us to visualize the effects of diverse sources of variations in a single chart.

When we understand where the most variation is occurring, we can focus our energies on identifying causes that contribute to that variation. Multivari studies should continue until the full range of the output variable is observed and all treatment combinations have been captured. (A *treatment* is a factor, or an X, and the level of the X is the *treatment level*.) If all treatment combinations have been observed and Y has not varied through its normal range, the Xs are not critical to Y. The goal of multivari is to reduce the large number of possible causes of variation to a smaller family of variation. This allows the team to focus on that family of variation.

You cannot know in advance how long it will take or exactly how many samples will be necessary to perform an appropriate multivari study. Typically, we start with a data collection sheet that makes sense based on our knowledge of the process. After the data are collected, we check to see if the variation in the study is similar to the variation observed from the process. If we see only minor variation in the sample, we go back and collect additional data.

For a multivari to work, the output must be continuous and the sources of variation must be discrete. For example, Figure 6-10 shows data from three typical sources of variation for a product-critical specification for pressure on a valve unit sold to a truck brake customer. The sources are within-piece variation, between-pieces variation, and over-time variation.

At first the chart looks fairly complex, with a lot of information about the problem. It's actually straightforward to interpret. First you need to show the specification limits for pressure in psi units—a lower spec limit of 53.5 psi and an upper spec limit of 56.5 psi.

The multivari chart indicates that the over-time variation (the diamond symbols in the oval) is within specifications and is not a major source of the problem. We are looking for data patterns that stand out. In the within-piece variation there appears to be a tight cluster of data points. However, the multivari chart clearly shows wide between-pieces variation, a strong indication that we should dive into the root causes here. We can also see that something good happened in the third panel, with the first set of within-piece data that we need to investigate as well, indicated by the down arrow.

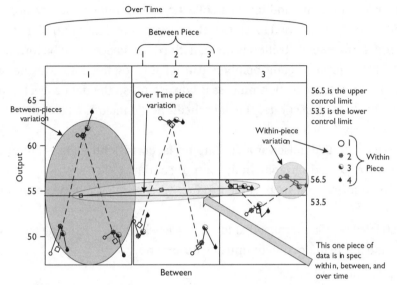

Figure 6-10. Multivari chart for output variation: between pieces, within a piece, and over-time

We look for patterns in the data. We want to see how variation within-piece, between-pieces, and over-time affect the valve pressure testing. Where is the most variation? Within-piece? Between-pieces? Over-time? Does the variation shown in the plot represent what we usually see in the process? You can always do a sanity check by using box plots or interval plots (discussed later) to confirm your interpretation of the multivari chart.

Here are the basic steps in multvari analysis:

Step 1. Call a team meeting and introduce the concepts of multivari analysis. Explain the purpose and the procedure for collecting and analyzing the data.

Step 2. Select the Xs to be included in the study. Potential Xs should come from the process map, the YX diagram, and/or the FMEA.

Step 3. Establish a sampling plan. Design the sampling plan to capture all relevant sources of variation. Multivari studies should continue until the full range of the output variable is observed and all treatment combinations have been captured. (Factors, or Xs, are the treatments, and the level of an X is the treatment level.)

Step 4. Plan the method for data collection. Determine which database fields need to be queried to capture the appropriate information for each record. If the data collection is manual, the data sheet should be formatted so that project team members can reliably log the data. This helps ensure the data collection process is consistent, so the data collected is more likely to be accurate. The data sheet should include a column for:

- Process Xs being evaluated;
- Uncontrolled noise variables (input that consistently causes random and expected variation in the output); and
- ID information, such as the product type, employee, time, location, etc.

Each level of a factor must include all the levels of the remaining factors. Provide a way to document unusual observations.

Step 5. Collect the data.

Step 6. Analyze the results.

Cause-and-Effect Diagrams

The *cause-and-effect diagram*, also known as *Ishikawa diagram* or *fishbone diagram* (Figure 6-11), is a simple but effective tool for identifying and mapping possible causes of a designated effect. Here's the procedure:

1. Define the effect, the problem.
2. Write the effect in a rectangle in the middle of the right side of a display area (e.g., flipchart or whiteboard) and draw a horizontal line to the left side of the display area. These are the "head" and "spine" of the "fishbone."
3. Brainstorm major categories of possible causes. Teams sometimes use generic categories, such as:
   - Methods (procedures, policies, requirements, regulations);
   - Machines (equipment, tools);
   - People (anyone involved in the process);
   - Materials (including parts and supplies);
   - Environment (conditions [including location, time temperature, humidity], culture); or

- Measurements (data from process used to assess performance).
4. Write the categories of causes as branches from both sides of the spine.
5. For each category, brainstorm all the possible causes. Write each cause as a branch from the appropriate category branch. (A cause may be put in more than one category.)
6. Brainstorm causes of the causes identified. Write each cause as a branch wherever appropriate.

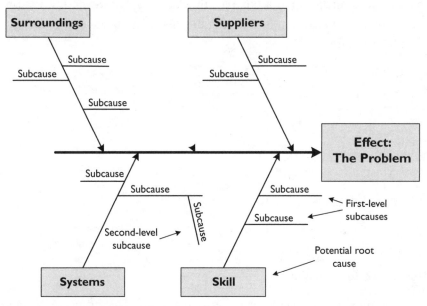

Figure 6-11. Cause-and-effect diagram

Interval Plots

The interval plot is a great graphical tool for comparing two or more factors. It is one of the more powerful house graphical tools you can use. Why? An *interval plot* represents the statistical significance of the *p-value*, which is the estimated probability of rejecting the null hypothesis in a statistical test

> ### INTERVAL PLOT
> A graphical summary of the distribution of a data sample that shows the central tendency and variability of the data, often with a symbol for the mean and a bar marking 95% confidence.
>
> **TOOLS**

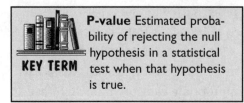

P-value Estimated probability of rejecting the null hypothesis in a statistical **KEY TERM** test when that hypothesis is true.

when that hypothesis is true. The p-value is the point at which feeling, thinking, and believing in what you know transfers to being 95% confident of a specific position.

The graph (Figure 6-12) shows the spread of data around the means of groups by plotting confidence intervals. In some cases an interval plot is easier to interpret than a box plot or a dot plot. However, it must be used with care, because it is graphing the 95% confidence end points by calculating them.

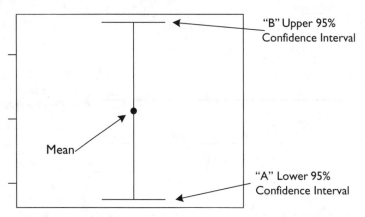

"B" Upper 95% Confidence Interval

Mean

"A" Lower 95% Confidence Interval

Figure 6-12. Interval plot

A confidence interval for specific statistics gives us a range of values around the statistic where the "true" (population) statistic is expected to be located with a given level of certainty. Most of the confidence is based on 1 minus the probability value (p-value), typically 5%, so the confidence is 95%. It's stated that you can conclude there's a 95% probability that the population mean is greater than A and less than B. If you set a lower p-value, then the interval becomes wider, thereby increasing the "certainty" of the estimate. If you set a higher p-value, the interval becomes narrower and the "certainty" decreases. It's like a weather forecast: The vaguer the prediction, that is, the wider the confidence interval, the more likely the prediction will be true. Note that the width of the confidence interval depends on the sample size and the variation of data values.

The calculation of confidence intervals is based on the assumption that the variable is distributed in the population normally. This estimate may not be valid if the assumption isn't valid, unless the sample size is large, say $n = 100$ or more. The calculation is based on the total distribution. Although the representation is similar to the layout of a box plot, it does *not* represent the data set, but rather the mean and standard deviation of the data set, which are used to calculate the confidence interval.

The following story is a real example from GE back in 1994. The weight of the agitator in a washing machine is a function of each of 10 mold cavities. If an agitator is incorrectly weighted, this defect can cause leaks; the correct weight is therefore a critical-to-quality characteristic for the customer. A correct weight means no warranty costs for repair and easier installation, no carpal tunnel syndrome in the operator, and only one person per shift required to install the agitator. Controlling these costs would result in $1 million in additional cash for GE.

The interval plot is the start of making statements about a hypothesis and percentage of risk or confidence in your conclusion. For example, "I am 95% confident that if I sample the weight of an agitator from mold cavity 1, it will be between 29.5 and 30.5 pounds, based on data that have been validated." Contrast this statement with "I think that cavity 1 is OK and much better than cavity 2."

The specification for a good agitator weight is between 29.5 and 30.5 pounds. We were 95% confident that the first four molding cavities (Figure 6-13) were going to produce properly weighted agitators. The other six were producing costly defects. This basic interval plot graphically proved that hypothesis of weight and isolated the problem at the supplier's location. It was enough proof to save the $1 million for GE. Containment did not address the root cause of the weight problem, but it was enough to sort the good and know what else needed to be done.

Time Series Plots

A *time series* is a sequence of measurements taken at successive points in time. It includes a wide range of exploratory and hypothesis-testing methods that have two main goals: (1) understand the phenomenon represented by the measurements and (2) predict future values of the variable tracked in the time series. Both goals require that we identify

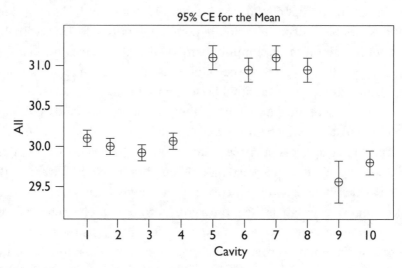

Figure 6-13. Interval plot, washing machine agitators

and describe more or less formally the pattern of time series data. We're looking for a pattern in the data that we can interpret and integrate with other data so we can use it in our hypothesis. We can validate our hypothesis by identifying and examining before-and-after trends. We can also extrapolate from any pattern we identify to predict future events.

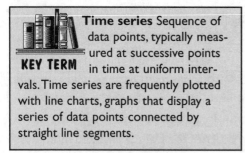

Time series Sequence of data points, typically measured at successive points in time at uniform intervals. Time series are frequently plotted with line charts, graphs that display a series of data points connected by straight line segments.

Most time series patterns can be described in terms of two basic categories: trend analysis and seasonality. *Trend analysis* is a time series plot that shows the data, the fitted trend line, and forecasts. Understanding your model is critical to the analysis. A model of the trend can be one of four main categories: linear, quadratic, exponential, and S-curve (where the trend starts slowly and moves up quickly to finally reach a plateau or flat line). *Seasonality analysis,* or *seasonal dependency,* is a time series pattern that shows a basic repetitive pattern over a long period, such as annual holiday sales for retailers. For the Analyze phase, the main concept to grasp is the defect rate over time, as shown in Figure 6-14.

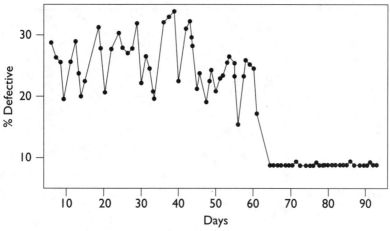

Figure 6-14. Times series plot: Defect rate over time

The plot clearly shows that somewhere around day 60, something changed that caused a reduction in defects. It clearly shows proof of a before-and-after trend.

Scatter Plots

A *scatter plot* is used to investigate the possible relationship between an independent variable (X) and a dependent variable (Y) by displaying data points in relation to a horizontal axis (X) and a vertical axis (Y).

Figure 6-15 is a scatter plot showing that an independent

> **SCATTER PLOT**
> Used to investigate the possible relationship between an independent variable (X) and a dependent variable (Y). The **TOOLS** plot displays data points in relation to a horizontal axis (X) and a vertical axis (Y). The scatter plot is the first step in doing a correlation and regression analysis.

variable, knob-A, may have an effect on the dependent variable, Y.

A scatter plot reveals a correlation: It's the first step toward doing a correlation and regression analysis. For example, this scatter plot (Figure 6-16) shows that when there's an increase in knob-A, there's an increase in Y.

The scatter plot often includes a straight *line of best fit*. This is a straight line that comes closest to all the data points on a scatter plot.

- If the data points cluster in a band from lower left to upper right, there's a positive correlation: If X increases, Y increases.

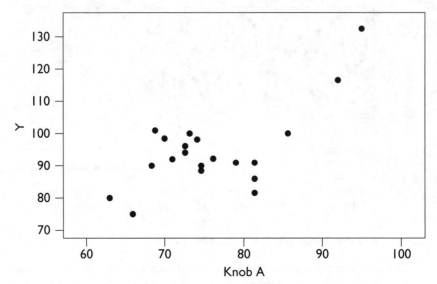

Figure 6-15. Scatter plot of Y and knob-A data points

- If the data points cluster in a band from upper left to lower right, there's a negative correlation: If X increases, Y decreases.
- The more closely the data points cluster around the line of best fit, the stronger the correlation, whether positive or negative.
- If the data points show no significant clustering, there's probably no correlation.

Figure 6-16 shows some scatter plots to guide you in interpreting plotted results.

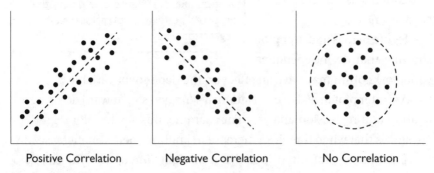

Positive Correlation   Negative Correlation   No Correlation

Figure 6-16. Scatter plots showing positive correlation, negative correlation, and no correlation

There's a fundamental rule in using scatter plots and correlation and regression tools: Correlation does not imply causation. A relationship does *not* mean there's a cause-and-effect connection. The correlation could be a coincidence.

> **Correlation** Relationship between variables that's greater than would be expected from chance alone, measured and expressed as a coefficient. *Linear correlation* occurs when two or more variables are related such that the data displayed on a scatter plot tends to cluster around a straight, nonhorizontal line.
>
> **KEY TERM**

We humans tend to see patterns and interconnections and we make assumptions. Don't assume: Test every correlation you find to determine whether it's causal or coincidental.

Hypothesis Testing

In the Analyze phase, the project team members determine which inputs affect the outputs of a process. The central activity of the Analyze phase is hypothesis testing. For each input (possible cause), the team members do the following:

Step 1. They develop two hypotheses (null and alternative).

Step 2. They test their hypotheses by analyzing data from the process.

Step 3. If their alternative hypothesis is correct, they add the input to a list of significant causes affecting the process.

There are many types of hypothesis tests, tests for comparison of both variable data and attribute data sets. It's always best to start with the types of risks that can be studied.

There are two types of hypothesis—a null hypothesis (H_0) and an alternative hypothesis (H_a or H_1). A null hypothesis (H_0) states the assumption that there's no difference in parameters for two or more populations, that any observed difference in samples is due to chance or a sampling error. It states, basically, "There is no difference in _____."

You would use a null hypothesis to check whether the new process mean differs from the old process mean. The test is to determine if any change in mean is due to random variation or if the process has changed and the new mean is significantly different from the old. The null hypothesis is assumed to be true until sufficient evidence is presented against it. The null hypothesis states that all the data belongs to the same underlying population, with the new process essentially equivalent to the old.

An alternative hypothesis (H_a or H_1) is any hypothesis that differs from a given null hypothesis. It states that the observed difference or relationship between two populations is real, that it's not the result of chance or a sampling error. While the null hypothesis is a statement of "no effect" or "no difference," an alternative hypothesis states that a difference or effect exists.

KEY TERMS

Null hypothesis (H_0) Hypothesis that sample observations result purely from chance.

Alternative hypothesis (H_a or H_1) Hypothesis that sample observations are influenced by some nonrandom cause.

Beta risk (β) Probability of accepting the null hypothesis (H_0) as true, when it's actually false. It's the risk of not discovering a difference in the sample characteristic of interest when a difference actually exists.

The *beta risk* (β) is the probability of accepting the null hypothesis (H_0) as true, when it's actually false. It's the risk of not discovering a difference in the sample characteristic of interest (e.g., the mean), when in reality such a difference does exist.

This is the statistical way to keep track—and it's also a reason to start hating statistics. Don't get lost by the designations; it's all about making comparisons!

A statistical hypothesis test is done by establishing two hypotheses, the null hypothesis and the alternative hypothesis, and then deciding which one to accept. It's akin to the concept of innocent until proven guilty: The null hypothesis assumes that the process parameter in question is not affected by what we did to change the process. In other words, any differences between the two data distributions initially are assumed to be due to random variation from one sampling of the process to another. Continuing the analogy, the alternative hypothesis bears the burden of proof that changing the process has led to a detectable change in its data distribution. The computations must lead to a high probability (rarely less than 90% and often much higher) that the change is real before we will accept the alternative hypothesis.

The decisions in a hypothesis test can be based on the probability value (p-value) for the given test. If the p-value is less than or equal to a predetermined level of significance (α-level), then you reject the null hypothesis and go with the alternative hypothesis. If your p-value is greater than the α-level, then you cannot reject the null hypothesis: There's no support for the alternative hypothesis.

When you perform a hypothesis test, there are four possible outcomes, summarized in Figure 6-17. The outcomes depend on whether the null hypothesis is true or false and whether you reject or fail to reject the null hypothesis.

Decision	Null Hypothesis Is True	Null Hypothesis Is False
Fail to reject null hypothesis	Correct decision	Type II error
Reject null hypothesis	Type I error	Correct decision

Figure 6-17. Hypothesis test: four possible outcomes

When the null hypothesis is true and you reject it, you make a type I error. The probability of making a type I error is called alpha (α) and is sometimes referred to as the level of significance. When the null hypothesis is false and you fail to reject it, you make a type II error. The probability of making a type II error is called beta (β).

Analysis of Variance (ANOVA)

The purpose of *analysis of variance (ANOVA)* is to test for significant differences between or among two or more means by comparing variances within groups and variances between and among groups. We use ANOVA to calculate the amount of variation in a process and determine if it's significant or if it's caused by *random noise*—input that consistently causes random and expected variation in the output.

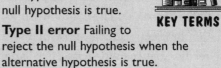

Type I error Rejecting the null hypothesis when the null hypothesis is true.

Type II error Failing to reject the null hypothesis when the alternative hypothesis is true.

KEY TERMS

> **ANALYSIS OF VARIANCE (ANOVA)**
> A test for significant differences between or among two or more
> means that compare variances within groups and variances
> between and among groups. It's used to calculate the amount of
> **TOOLS**   variation in a process and determine if it's significant or if it's
> caused by random noise—input that consistently causes random
> and expected variation in the output.

Specifically, by partitioning the total variation into different sources (associated with the different effects in the design), we are able to compare the variance due to variability between or among groups or treatments with the variance due to variability within a group or a treatment. (As mentioned earlier, a treatment is a property or characteristic that allows us to distinguish one population from another.) Under the null hypothesis (there are no differences in mean between or among groups or treatments in the population) the variance estimated from the variability within the group or treatment should be about the same as the variance estimated from the variability between or among groups or treatments.

There are two types of analysis of variance. *One-way ANOVA* allows comparisons of several groups of observations, all of which are independent but possibly with a different mean for each group. *Two-way ANOVA* is a way to study the main effects of two factors separately and, sometimes, together (the effects of their interaction).

Before we go too far, we need to explain *statistical significance* (p-level), which we mentioned earlier in the context of interval plots and confidence intervals. The statistical significance (p-level) of a result is an estimated measure of the degree to which it is "true"—representative of the population. More technically, the value of the p-level represents a decreasing index of the reliability of a result. The higher the p-level, the less we can believe that the relation between variables observed in the sample is a reliable indicator of the relation between the respective variables in the population. Specifically, the p-level represents the probability of error involved in accepting our observed result as valid, that is, representative of the population.

For example, as shown Figure 6-18, the p-level of 0.05 (i.e., 1/20) indicates there's a 5% probability that the relation between the variables

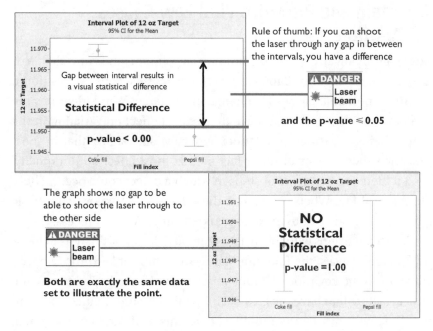

Figure 6-18. Interval plot and rules of statistical significance in a visual format

found in our sample is a fluke. In other words, assuming that in the population there was no relation between those variables and we repeated our experiment again and again, we could expect that in approximately every 20 replications of the experiment there would be one in which the relation between the variables in question would be equal to or stronger than the relation found in the first test. The p-value of 0.05 is customarily treated as a borderline acceptable error level; that is, if the p-value is less than the acceptable target of 0.05, you have a statistical significance event or there's a difference in the data comparison.

If a factor is a common cause and it contributes significantly to variability in the output, the team has an opportunity to improve the process by controlling the factor. If the primary sources of variation are special causes, uncontrollable, and significant, the team may decide to recommend redesigning the process to withstand that variability to the degree possible or abandoning the project. If any sources of variation are uncontrollable but the team assesses their effect as minor, the team may continue with the project but adjust its goals.

Ascertain and Prioritize Vital Few Causes of Variation

After identifying any causes of variation as common and controllable or as special and uncontrollable, the team narrows its focus. At this point, it screens potential causes for change in the target Y and identifies the vital few Xs—the inputs that have the greatest effect on variation in the output being measured in relation. Typically, data shows that in most processes there are six or fewer factors that most affect output quality, even if there are hundreds of steps in which a defect could occur. These are the vital few. When you isolate these factors, you know what basic adjustments you need to make to markedly improve the process.

The team begins with the insights gained in its initial analysis to identify the root causes, the fundamental relationships of key process input variables to the key process input variables under study. To identify the critical factors that have the greatest influence on performance, the team uses the Five Whys, cause-and-effect diagrams, and Pareto charts. Then, to confirm that it will focus on the vital few root causes of variation, the team uses hypothesis testing and Design of Experiments.

FIVE WHYS

TOOLS

A technique used to probe the cause-and-effect relationships underlying a problem. The primary objective is to determine the problem's root cause. First ask, "Why?" about the problem and then ask, "Why?" in response to the answer. The questioning could continue beyond five "Whys," but experience has shown that five are generally enough to determine a root cause. It's most important to focus on the process: Why did the process fail? The answer should never be people. People do not fail; processes fail.

To estimate the impact of each X on Y and prioritize the causes, the black belt develops theories about possible causes and then uses data to confirm or disprove those theories. The tools provide insights into the relationships between the key process input variables and the key process output variables.

To verify its findings, the team gathers additional data and may conduct experiments on the process, making certain changes to see if the problems disappear or using pilot testing to try the changes on a small scale to see if they improve the results.

To determine the key input variables that cause the target output variables to vary and then to prioritize those inputs, the team can use ANOVA, analysis of means (ANOM), F-test, t-test, chi-square test, and/or Design of Experiments.

What are these tools?

- *ANOM* is a statistical procedure for analyzing the results of experimental designs with factors at fixed levels and providing a graphical display of data. ANOM was developed as an alternative to ANOVA and is easier to use because it's an extension of the control chart.
- An *F-test* determines whether two samples drawn from different populations have the same standard deviation, with a specified confidence level.
- A *t-test* determines whether the averages of normally distributed population samples differ from each other with statistical confidence.
- The *chi-square test*, the most popular hypothesis testing method for discrete (count) data, uses a matrix to look for statistical differences among populations. The test consists of three types of analysis:
  1. Test for *goodness of fit*, which determines if the sample being analyzed was drawn from a population that follows some specified distribution.
  2. Test for *homogeneity*, which shows that the populations being analyzed are homogeneous in terms of some characteristic.
  3. Test for *independence*, which tests the null hypothesis that two criteria of classification are independent when applied to a population of subjects.

The team can check the root causes against the critical outputs using an association matrix, helping the team prioritize possible solutions to develop for the root causes associated with the highest-priority outputs. The team creates a table in which it lists the root causes across the top and the possible solutions down the left side. Then the team discusses and determines the potential of each solution to reduce or eliminate the effects of each root cause and marks the potential in the associated cell. The $Y = f(X)$ relationships that the team identifies, verifies, and quantifies as the vital few form the basis for the solutions in the Improve phase.

In this step the team can also use multivari analysis and failure modes and effects analysis (FMEA; discussed in Chapter 5).

To know how the inputs affect the process output capabilities, the team uses multivari analysis to identify the significant inputs, characterize the process, and identify the inherent capabilities and limitations of a process.

First, the team gets data samples, using one or more methods of representative sampling—random, systematic, subgroup, and cluster or stratified sampling. Multivari analysis of the samples generates a chart that presents an analysis of the variation in the process in its normal state by differentiating three main sources:

1. intrapiece (variation within a piece, batch, or lot);
2. interpiece (variation from piece to piece); or
3. temporal (variation related to time).

The team then graphs the interrelationship of multiple variables in the process to determine which variable contributes the most to that variation, using a multivari plot, a box plot, a main effects plot, or a regression plot.

The team can compare input variables and output variables. It can also quantify basic correlation by using regression (the relationship between the mean value of a random variable and the corresponding values of one or more independent variables) with the data from the multivari analysis to determine the formula that correlates input variables and output variables. Sometimes a multivari analysis reveals the causes of variations; in other cases, the outputs of a multivari analysis become the inputs for a factorial experiment.

Transform the Gaps into Improvement Projects

Now the team identifies ways to reduce or close the gaps between the current performance and the potential to improve the process. First, team members prioritize the opportunities to improve the process. Which problems should they solve to achieve the greatest gains? Then they generate alternatives, evaluate those alternatives, and select the best solutions. Next, they identify potential problems and obstacles they might encounter in implementing those solutions.

Once they've mapped out what they want to do and any problems and obstacles, they decide on the necessary people and resources to improve the process.

Finally, the team translates the improvement opportunity into financial terms. There are three questions to answer:

1. What's the cost of poor quality that the team intends to save by implementing the solutions?
2. What's the investment in people and resources that the improvement will require?
3. What will be the financial gain in terms of ROI or a cost-benefit analysis?

Review the Project with the Champion

The black belt meets with the champion to discuss the project's Analyze phase, to prepare for the phase-gate review that concludes this phase. Here are some questions they may discuss:

- Has the team identified and verified the variation's root causes?
- As a result of knowledge gained during the Analyze phase, should the team update the problem statement, project goals, and/or business case?
- Has the team identified any unexpected benefits that will result from closing or reducing all or most of the gaps?
- Are there any significant factors the team should further investigate in the Improve phase?

Conduct an Analyze Phase-Gate Review

At the end of the Analyze phase, just as in the Define and Measure phases, the black belt should report to the executive leaders on the project's status. The report should cover such general questions as:

- How has the team identified potential Xs? Which tools did the team use (e.g., process maps, histograms, box plots, dot plots, multivari analysis, cause-and-effect diagrams, interval plots, time series plots, scatter plots)? What were the results?
- What data does the team have to verify the Xs it has identified? Which

tools did the team use (e.g., regression analysis, hypothesis testing, analysis of variance)? What were the results?

- Has the team ascertained and prioritized the vital few causes of process variation?
- Has the team developed a preliminary $Y = f(X)$ equation to use in the Improve phase?
- Has the problem statement or objective changed? If so, how should the project charter be modified?
- Is the project on track to meet the scheduled completion date? If not, why not? What could be done to make more progress in less time?
- Are the team members satisfied with the cooperation and support they're getting from others in the organization? If not, how could cooperation and support be improved?

Beyond presenting the results of the Analyze phase and answering questions from the executive leaders, the black belt may use this opportunity to make suggestions, address problems, or request additional resources.

Manager's Checklist for Chapter 6

☑ The purpose of the Analyze phase is to evaluate and reduce the variables, using graphical analysis and hypothesis testing, and to identify the vital few factors in order to identify the root cause(s) of the defects.

☑ The Analyze phase is a major transition into using data to know rather than relying on feeling, thinking, and believing.

☑ The project team should use whatever tools will help it sort through all potential Xs to link a vital few factors to the most important and costly defects.

☑ The interval plot is a useful tool for distinguishing between good and bad performance.

☑ At the end of the Analyze phase, the project team should have identified and verified the root causes of variation and the significant factors to be further investigated in the Improve phase.

☑ It's always a good idea to revisit the problem statement, project goals, and business case to ensure their continuing validity.

Improve Phase

> To improve is to change; to be perfect is to have changed often.
> —Winston Churchill (1874-1965)

This phase is usually initiated by selecting those product or process performance characteristics that must be improved to achieve the goal. Those characteristics are then diagnosed to reveal the major sources of variation. Next, the key process input variables (Xs) are identified through statistically designed experiments. Proven process variables that have been filtered through the Analyze phase and are identified as the vital few Xs are included in the experiment. The goal now is to form the $Y = f(X)$ relationship to be leveraged and to establish performance specifications.

The role of a statistically designed experiment is to identify the most influential factors (vital few) associated with a particular critical-to-quality (CTQ) characteristic and to define their relationships using analytical quantities. Since interactions between and among various factors are also defined, a single Design of Experiments (DOE) can yield many revealing facts, allowing the experimenters to quickly improve the process. The DOE analysis also specifically indicates what percent of each factor is contributing to the output and how much of the error (difference from the expected results) cannot be explained. The larger the error, the less you know about the process or product defect.

In the Improve phase, the team should be ready to develop, test, and implement solutions to improve the process by reducing the variation in the critical output variables caused by the vital few input variables. The team must demonstrate, with data, that its solutions work. In this phase, the team members generate ideas for improving the process, analyze and evaluate those ideas, select and test the best potential solutions, plan and implement the solutions, then validate the results with data and statistical analysis.

Thomas Pyzdek, an author on Six Sigma, makes an important point:

> To some extent, the Analyze and Improve phases are conducted simultaneously. In fact, there is Improvement in every phase of the project. The work done in the Define, Measure, and Analyze phases all help better determine what the customer wants, how to measure it, and what the existing process can do to provide it. (Thomas Pyzdek, *The Six Sigma Project Planner: A Step-by-Step Guide to Leading a Six Sigma Project Through DMAIC*, New York, NY: McGraw-Hill, 2001.)

So, Pyzdek states, a team may make enough improvement in the first three phases that it meets the project goals before reaching the Improve phase. If that happens, the decision may be made to end the project. However, this situation is rare. Generally, teams follow the steps outlined below.

Improve Phase Activities

The Improve phase consists of the following basic steps. The outline here is generic; the champion and the black belt must modify these steps as appropriate to the specific project.

The team continues to check for relationships among the vital few Xs and between the Xs and the Y, as in the Analyze phase. Tests may be necessary to understand any interactions among the input variables and to analyze the variation contributed by each component to see if one component is causing most of the variation in the target outputs. The team uses Design of Experiments (DOE), analysis of variance (ANOVA), and regression analysis.

Improve Phase Tools

In the Improve phase, the project team uses these major tools, which are discussed in this chapter:

- Correlation and regression analysis
- Design of Experiments (DOE)

A discussion of this phase could include many more tools and activities, but the thrust of this chapter is to show what happens in the Improve phase and not all the activities a project team could carry out, as they depend on the specific situation.

Correlation

When we analyze the data collected during the Measure phase, it's important to be able to reliably determine if a relationship exists between process/product inputs and process/product outputs and to measure the strength of that relationship.

Correlation is the relation between or among two or more variables, measured and expressed as a coefficient. Correlation coefficients can range from +1.00 to −1.00. A value of +1.00 represents a perfect positive correlation; a value of −1.00 represents a perfect negative correlation; a value of 0.00 represents a lack of correlation (see Figure 6-17).

> **Correlation coefficient**
> Measure of correlation, between +1.00 and −1.00. **KEY TERM**
> A value of +1.00 represents a perfect positive correlation; a value of −1.00 represents a perfect negative correlation; a value of 0.00 represents a lack of correlation.

The basics of correlations are these:

1. Correlation aids in establishing $Y = f(X)$.
2. Correlation is a measure of strength of association between two quantitative variables (e.g., pressure and yield).
3. Correlation measures the degree of linearity between two variables.
4. Correlation is expressed as a coefficient between +1 and −1.
5. A positive coefficient indicates a positive correlation; a negative coefficient indicates a negative correlation.

6. Rule: A correlation > 0.80 is important; a correlation < 0.20 is not significant. However, be careful with sample size.

7. The coefficient of linear correlation "r" is the measure of the strength.

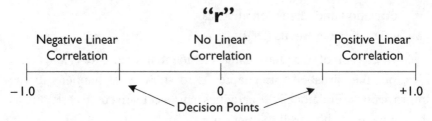

Figure 7-1. Correlation continuum

The type of data to be collected for a correlation must be bivariate. *Bivariate data* describes two pieces of data that are variable. Expressed mathematically, bivariate data constitutes ordered pairs; let's call them X and Y (X, Y). It's customary to call the input variable (independent) X and the output variable (dependent) Y.

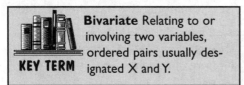

Bivariate Relating to or involving two variables, ordered pairs usually designated X and Y.

KEY TERM

Another basic is that correlation does not imply causation. We humans tend to see patterns and interconnections, especially if they support something we believe. This tendency is known as confirmation bias. We tend to confuse coincidence with correlation and to confuse correlation with causality. Don't assume: Make sure that any correlation you establish is causal.

The correlation continuum (Figure 7-1) shows two decision points (also known as critical values), where the value of the correlation coefficient indicates whether the correlation is significant. The decision points determine the strength of the correlation between two variables. As mentioned in the list of correlation basics above, the rule of thumb is that any correlation > 0.80 is important and any correlation < 0.20 is not significant. But you need to consider the size of your data sample (and a few other values that are beyond the scope of this discussion).

As the data size (expressed as *n*) increases, the value of the decision point decreases, as shown in a decision points table (Figure 7-2). (If the coefficient is negative, disregard the minus sign when using this table.)

If the coefficient is less than or equal to the decision point for the sample size, then we cannot be sure whether a correlation exists between two variables. If the coefficient is greater than the decision point, then there is some correlation.

Sample Size (n)	Decision Point	Sample Size (n)	Decision Point	Sample Size (n)	Decision Point
5	0.878	16	0.497	40	0.312
6	0.811	17	0.482	50	0.279
7	0.754	18	0.468	60	0.254
8	0.707	19	0.456	70	0.232
9	0.666	20	0.444	80	0.220
10	0.632	21	0.433	90	0.205
11	0.602	22	0.423	100	0.196
12	0.576	23	0.413	200	0.139
13	0.553	24	0.404	300	0.113
14	0.532	25	0.396	400	0.098
15	0.514	30	0.514	500	0.098

Figure 7-2. Decision points table, showing sample size (*n*) and decision point

The usual measure of linear correlation is the Pearson correlation coefficient. The *Pearson correlation coefficient* (also called *Pearson r* or *product-moment correlation*) determines the extent to which the values of two variables are proportional (related linearly) to each other.

This is the formula for Pearson r:

$$r = \frac{\Sigma(x-\bar{x})(y-\bar{y})}{(n-1)s_1 s_2}$$

Statistical software such as Minitab or Excel will do these calculations for you.

Regression Analysis

Regression (discussed briefly in Chapter 6) is a statistical measure that determines the strength of the relationships between a dependent or response variable (Y) and one or more independent or predictor variables (Xs). The goal is to determine the values of parameters for a function that cause that function to best fit a set of data observations. Regression analysis is one of the more widely used data analysis methods, a technique for investigating and modeling the relationship between variables.

The discussion of correlation above is based on determining the relationship between a single X and a Y. This is simple linear regression. For more than one X, which is the usual situation, the process is multiple linear regression.

Regression analysis consists of two steps. First, the team identifies the dependent variable Y it wants to predict. Then the team carries out multiple regression analysis that focuses on the independent variables it wants to use as predictors or explanatory variables, the Xs. The analysis identifies the relationship between the Y and the Xs as a mathematical formula, a model.

There are regression tools to examine both linear and nonlinear relationships. In linear regression, the function is a straight-line equation. In other words, regression analysis fits a straight line to data points so they are distributed evenly along the line, which creates a simplified, often accurate representation of the relationships. In nonlinear (curvilinear) regression, the relationship is described by a curve, not a straight line.

We don't get into the complexities of regression analysis here. Black belts are the experts in regression analysis and they use statistical tools in software such as Minitab. You need to understand the fundamentals so you can understand what the black belt is doing.

Here's the formula for a simple linear regression, which describes the relationship between the dependent output variable (Y) and the independent input variable (X):

$$Y = b_0 + b_1 X$$

This equation states that the Y variable can be expressed in terms of a constant (b_0) and a slope (b_1) times the X variable. The constant is also known as the intercept or Y-intercept; it's the value of Y when X is zero. The slope is the regression coefficient, which specifies how much Y will change when X changes by one unit.

The simplest regression occurs when there's only one X related to Y. Multiple linear regression models are more complicated because there are two or more Xs. Then the equation shown above expands and becomes more complicated. In addition to the main effects (the effect of each X on Y), there's the consideration of interactions between and among the Xs.

Constant in regression The value of output Y when input X is zero. Also known as intercept or **KEY TERMS** Y-intercept.

Slope in regression The coefficient, which specifies how much Y will change when X changes by one unit.

Effect (of a factor) Difference between the mean of all data points obtained when the factor is set at its high level and the mean of all data points obtained when the factor is set at its low level.

Design of Experiments

An *experiment* is a systematic procedure, conducted under controlled conditions, to discover or study an effect or to test or develop a hypothesis. Specifically, when we analyze a process, we experiment with the process to identify the inputs that have a significant effect on the output and determine what the inputs must be to produce the output we want.

To design an experiment, we must first clearly understand the process and decide which factor we want to investigate. Once the experiment is complete, we will better understand what's important and we can design another experiment. We do this until we obtain the desired result.

There are several ways to construct and conduct experiments to test the effects of variables. The traditional approach is to change only one variable at a time, holding the other variables constant. This one-factor-

Design of Experiments (DOE) A structured way to conduct controlled tests and analyze the **KEY TERM** results to evaluate the independent or predictor variables (Xs) that affect a dependent or response variable (Y). The design techniques enable those using DOE to determine simultaneously the individual and interactive effects of the Xs on the Y.

at-a-time approach works well when there are few variables, but for more complex situations it can take a lot of time and is considered an inefficient approach to problem solving. That's why Design of Experiments (DOE) was developed. For exploring complex problems, DOE is a more efficient approach than running a series of experiments, each testing a single factor, because DOE allows us to test all factors at the same time.

The objective of DOE is to minimize time and costs by minimizing the number of tests, yet study as many factors as possible to identify the important ones. DOE is a structured way to conduct controlled tests and analyze the results to evaluate the independent or predictor variables (Xs) that affect a dependent or response variable (Y). The design techniques enable us to determine simultaneously the individual and interactive effects of the Xs on the Y.

Even if a factor's main effect is not statistically significant, the factor may affect the output via interaction with another factor. We should consider both the main effects and the interactions when specifying optimal settings for a process. Two-factor interactions are common. There may also be *higher-order interactions* (interactions among three or more independent variables), but those are rare in most industries, with exceptions such as complex chemical industrial experiments.

We want to identify the factors that affect mean, variation, or both or that have no effect on the Y. Then we want to optimize the levels of the important factors to produce the desired response.

A DOE has three components: design experiment, carry out experiment, and analyze procedure. To produce the best results, it's best to prepare the plan and the analysis carefully before conducting the experiment.

Several types of DOE can be used, depending on how well a process is understood. DOEs are generally classified in one of three designs.

1. *Screening* designs are typically used early in the process to test many factors (typically, more than five) to identify the vital few factors on which to focus.
2. *Characterization* designs narrow the factors to only a few and allow for quantitative understanding of the interrelationships and interactions.
3. *Optimization* designs focus on only one or two factors, but in greater depth, to gain a precise understanding of the relationships.

Figure 7-3 shows a process for manufacturing injection-molded parts, with multiple output characteristics (Ys) and multiple input factors (Xs).

Inputs (Xs)	Process	Outputs (Ys)
Type of raw material	**Process**	Thickness of molded part
Mold temperature		Percent shrinkage from
Holding pressure	Manufacturing	mold size
Gate size	Injection-Molded	Percent defects
Screw speed	Parts	Weight of molded part
Percent regrind		
Moisture content		

Figure 7-3. Process for manufacturing injection-molded parts

The equation for the thickness of the molded part is a function of what factors? How do you set the inputs to obtain the thickness and weight you need to meet specs? How do you make the thickness and weight stable? Which input(s) need adjustment at what setting(s) to minimize shrinkage? The purpose of DOE and the Improve phase is to uncover the answers to these questions.

Planning the Experiment (DOE)

Planning is the most important piece of the DOE process. The analysis is straightforward and takes about 10–20% of the time for the entire experiment. We will now look at the basics of this method and some essential terms.

Full Factorial Design

A *full factorial design* combines two levels for each factor with two levels for every other factor. A *level* is a value or a setting for a factor, an assignment of high or low for each input variable (X) being tested. For example, a voltage may be set at 3.2 volts (low) or 5.4 volts (high), a temperature may be set at 95º (low) or 120º (high), a process time may be set at 20 minutes (low) or 35 minutes (high), and so on. In general, factor levels should be set wide, but not so much that they extend beyond the factor's operational range.

The notation used to char-

> **Full factorial design** A DOE design in which all possible combinations of the levels of the factors are investigated.

KEY TERM

acterize a DOE two-level experiment is 2^k, where k is the number of factors being tested. A full factorial design would require 2^k runs. So, for example, for a two-level experiment testing two factors, 2^2, a full factorial design would require four runs, as shown in the design matrix in Figure 7-4.

Run	Factor A	Factor B
I	Low (−)	Low (−)
2	Low (−)	High (+)
3	High (+)	Low (−)
4	High (+)	High (+)

Figure 7-4. Design matrix for a two-level test of two input variables

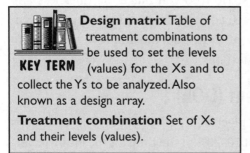

Design matrix Table of treatment combinations to be used to set the levels **KEY TERM** (values) for the Xs and to collect the Ys to be analyzed. Also known as a design array.

Treatment combination Set of Xs and their levels (values).

Experiment runs are calculated through the use of a *design matrix* (also known as an *array*), a table of treatment combinations that are used to set the levels (values) for the Xs and to collect the Ys to be analyzed. A treatment combination is a set of Xs and their levels (values). In a design matrix, a treatment combination is one row of Xs (input variables) and their corresponding levels that directly correspond to the Y or output in the same row. The levels or settings are generally written as − or −1 (low) and + or +1 (high) in constructing the design and then as the actual settings.

A 2^3 (2 to the third) experiment involves three variables, each at two levels. There are $2^3 = 8$ possible combinations, or total runs. Figure 7-5 shows the design array for this full factorial.

A 2^4 (2 to the fourth) experiment involves four variables, each at two levels. There are $2^4 = 16$ possible combinations.

The design matrix is generally organized according to *Yates order*, which is the standard. Here's how it works. As explained above, k is the number of factors. The kth column consists of 2^{k-1} minus signs (the low level of the factor) followed by 2^{k-1} plus signs (the high level of the factor).

Run	Factor A	Factor B	Factor C
1	– 1	– 1	– 1
2	– 1	– 1	+1
3	– 1	+1	– 1
4	– 1	+1	+1
5	+1	– 1	– 1
6	+1	– 1	+1
7	+1	+1	– 1
8	+1	+1	+1

Figure 7-5. Design matrix for a two-level test of three input variables

This order gives us, for a full factorial design with three factors, the design matrix in Figure 7-5.

One of the objectives in a DOE is to determine the effect of each factor (X) on the response variable (Y) and on the total variation of that variable, independent of the effects of the other factors. A good DOE design is orthogonal. Othogonality is a property of a DOE matrix in which the factors are independent.

A design matrix is orthogonal if it's balanced both vertically and horizontally. Vertical balancing occurs if the effects of any factor balance (if

---

Yates order Standard order for organizing the treatment combinations in a DOE design matrix. With k being the number of factors, the kth column consists of 2^{k-1} minus signs (the low level of the factor) followed by 2^{k-1} plus signs (the high level **KEY TERM** of the factor). Yates order is a basic organization structure of combinations in a sequential order. For example, here is a 2^3 full factorial or all combinations of a two-level, three-factor DOE matrix:

```
–  –  –
+  –  –
–  +  –
+  +  –
–  –  +
+  –  +
–  +  +
+  +  +
```

the number of pluses and minuses in each column are the same), as in Figure 7-5, where each factor is tested at four high settings and four low settings. Horizontal balancing occurs when the sum of the products of the corresponding rows in two columns is zero. A design is horizontally balanced if each two-column combination totals zero.

The design matrix in Figure 7-6 is orthogonal, that is, it's balanced both vertically and horizontally. For each factor, there are equal numbers of high and low values (vertical balance). For each level within each factor (each row in the matrix, i.e., each treatment combination), the "product" of multiplying the positives and negatives is a value that causes the row to total zero. There are equal numbers of high and low values (horizontal balance).

Run	A	B	C	Horizontal Product	
1	–	–	–	–	$(-) \times (-) \times (-) =$ negative
2	–	–	+	+	$(-) \times (-) \times (+) =$ positive
3	–	+	–	+	$(-) \times (+) \times (-) =$ positive
4	–	+	+	–	$(-) \times (+) \times (+) =$ negative
5	+	–	–	+	$(+) \times (-) \times (-) =$ positive
6	+	–	+	–	$(+) \times (-) \times (+) =$ negative
7	+	+	–	–	$(+) \times (+) \times (-) =$ negative
8	+	+	+	+	$(+) \times (+) \times (+) =$ positive
Sum of Product	0	0	0	0	

Vertical Sum

Figure 7-6. Design matrix showing orthogonality

If we want to test four factors, 2^4, a full factorial design would mean 16 runs. To test 10 factors, 2^{10}, we would need to carry out 1,024 runs (see Figure 7-7).

A full factorial design would be best, theoretically, because the design would cover all the combinations and provide the best data. However, it

Factors (k)	Runs (2^k)
2	4
3	8
4	16
5	32
6	64
7	128
8	256
9	512
10	1024

Figure 7-7. Table showing number of factors and number of runs

also could take a lot of time and resources—and produce a lot of defects. Fortunately, we can reduce the number of experimental runs by *fractioning the design,* a common practice of carrying out a fractional factorial experiment when there are five or more factors.

Fractional Factorial Design

A *fractional factorial design* is a DOE design in which only some of all possible combinations of the levels of the factors are investigated. Designs can be a half fraction, a quarter fraction, or an eighth fraction of a full factorial design. In a fractional factorial design, the team excludes some treatment combinations. Doing a half fraction, a quarter fraction, or an eighth fraction of a full factorial design can greatly reduce the time and cost needed to run a full factorial experiment. The number of experimental runs must be a power of 2 (4, 8, 16, 32, 64, etc.).

As mentioned earlier, a full factorial design for k factors at two levels is represented as 2^k. A fractional factorial design for k factors at two levels is represented as 2^{k-1}. For example, if we use three factors, it would be 2^{3-1}, or 2^2, and there would be four runs, not eight. This is half the number of the full factorial, so it's a half fractional factorial experiment.

In addition to the half fraction, it's also possible to do a quarter fraction or an eighth fraction of a full factorial design. If we want to study six factors at two levels, a full factorial design means 64 runs. But maybe we

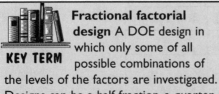

Fractional factorial design A DOE design in which only some of all possible combinations of the levels of the factors are investigated. Designs can be a half fraction, a quarter fraction, or an eighth fraction of a full factorial design.

could study the six factors well enough with 32 runs (half fraction), 16 runs (quarter fraction), or even 8 runs (eighth fraction). Figure 7-8 shows the design array for a half fractional factorial.

This half fractional factorial design is balanced, that is, for each factor there are equal numbers of high and low values in each factor column and for each treatment combination. The "product" of multiplying the positives and negatives is a value that causes the row to sum to zero. This design collapses into a full factorial. In other words, should any factor turn out not to matter, the result is a full factorial for the other factors. The design covers much of the region of interest with only half the runs. If the experiment uses expensive equipment or takes a long time, the team can reduce the cost by almost half. If it's possible to get the same information from fewer runs, it's worth considering a fractional factorial experiment.

For a fractional factorial design, determining the Yates order requires knowledge of the confounding structure of the design. Confounding is fundamental to the construction of fractional factorial designs. Con-

Combination	Factor A Setting	Factor B Setting	Factor C Setting
1	-1	-1	-1
3	-1	1	-1
5	1	-1	-1
7	1	1	-1

Figure 7-8. Design array for a 2^{3-1} (2^2) fractional factorial experiment

founding in this context means intentionally sacrificing the ability to identify and understand some effects and/or interactions. This trade-off is based on the principle that responses are usually affected by a small number of main effects (effects of a single independent variable) and lower-order interactions (i.e., between two independent variables) and that higher-order interactions (i.e., among three or more independent variables) are relatively unimportant.

Fractional factorial designs are used to screen experiments during their initial stages, when the project team needs to investigate a large number of factors and the focus is on the main effects and two-factor interactions. These designs obtain information about main effects and lower-order interactions with fewer runs by confounding these effects with unimportant higher-order interactions.

Replications

When the design or the results call for an experiment to be run more than once, the subsequent run may be either a *repetition* or a *replication*. For a *repetition*, the factors are not reset: it's simply a repeat run. For a *replication*, the factors are reset. *Replicates* tend to provide a better estimate of experimental error, but they cost more. Be sure to not overlook the economics.

Replications in a DOE depend on the problem we're trying to solve. For example, if we have a spread or variation problem beyond the specification, we must replicate to analyze the cause of the variation, not just the centering or mean of the problem. If we replicate once, the only way we can analyze the variation is by the measure of spread using range, the difference between the lowest and highest values. To calculate standard deviation to measure variation, we need at least three data points. More replication is better when trying to solve a spread or dispersion problem. If you have five replications, then you could analyze the standard deviation of Y. The replication of five would show not only the fac-

> **Confounding** Indication that the value of a main effect estimate comes from both the main effect and **KEY TERM** contamination or bias from higher-order interactions. Confounding happens naturally whenever a fractional factorial design is used instead of a full factorial design.

> **KEY TERM**
>
> **Replication** Complete repetition of the same experimental conditions, beginning with the initial setup, without changing any factor settings. Replication increases the sample size and is a way to increase the experiment's precision, estimate the noise (experimental error) in the system so as to determine whether observed differences in the data are real, and be better able to identify smaller effects.

tors causing the centering problem, but also the factors causing the dispersion problem.

Sometime the DOE economics prevent the replication. For example, if you are crashing cars into a cement wall and evaluating the effects of five factors at two setting levels with five replications, this would be 2^5 times, which is 32 combinations time 5 replicates, which would result in 160 cars. At $20,000 a car, 160 runs would cost $3,200,000. Wow! You definitely need to do good hypothesis testing during the Analyze phase to design your experiment most efficiently. (Of course, in any situation where the problem involves safety, the business needs to do the right thing.)

Randomization

The runs of treatment combinations are most often organized in the design matrix in standard order during planning and then during analysis, because it's logical, but "organized" in random order when the experiment is run.

The runs shouldn't be performed in the standard order or any other chosen order because of the possibility that the effects of one or more variables will be confused with the effects of one or more lurking variables. These are uncontrolled and unobserved variables that change during the experiment and might affect the response.

Randomizing the order of the runs doesn't protect against all effects of lurking variables, but randomization should be part of any experiment design. However, this is also a question of time and money. Do you have the resources to possibly change all your factor settings after every run?

To ensure that a DOE is designed correctly, the black belt must consider such items as Yates order, factor levels (using the –1 and +1 notation), balanced orthogonality, confounding, and interactions between and among factors. Also, there are design factors that influence the time and cost of the DOE, such as replications and design type.

The two-level, two-factor design is common and a good starting point for most problems. When replications are taken into account, meaningful results can be achieved with as few as 8–16 runs. When you don't know which factor has a substantial effect on a response variable and you want to verify several factors, then the fractional factorial design is preferred.

> **Lurking variable** Variable that has an important effect on the response but isn't among the variables studied in the experiment. The effects of lurking variables can be confused with the effects of the variables selected for the experiment.
>
> **KEY TERM**

It's common practice to do a fractional factorial experiment when there are five or more factors, because it requires fewer runs. For example, a six-factor, two-level experiment with no replications would involve 64 runs. The team can reduce this number if it runs experiments that represent only a portion of the matrix.

Fractional factorial designs are useful for screening factors because they reduce the number of runs. However, there are disadvantages. If you don't run all factor-level combinations, some of the effects of those factors may be confounded, mixed together so that the effects can't be estimated separately. In DOE terms, the effects are *aliased*: It's impossible to determine which factor is causing which effect.

One way to measure alias-

> **INVEST IN KNOWLEDGE**   **SMART**
>
>
>
> The project team tests settings of input variables on output variables, and the experiments cause defects. Man-   **MANAGING**
> agers may be apprehensive about the defects that result from experimentation, but they should realize and accept that the cost of those defects is an investment in learning how to reduce or eliminate the problem. The cost of learning is lower than the cost of not knowing how to improve processes.

> **STAY FOCUSED ON YOUR PURPOSE**   **CAUTION**
>
> "The purpose of an experiment is to better understand the real world, not to understand the experimental data." — William Diamond, *Practical Experiment Designs for Engineers and Scientists*.
>
> Remember this major truth, as you want to make real-world changes to gain a financial benefit.

ing in two-level designs is called *resolution*. The resolution of a design indicates how the effects are confounded. Resolution is typically measured as III or higher, with a higher number indicating less significant aliasing. Here are some common design resolutions:

- Resolution III: No main effect is aliased with any other main effect, but main effects are aliased with two-factor interactions and two-factor interactions are aliased with each other.
- Resolution IV: No main effect is aliased with any other main effect or two-factor interaction, but two-factor interactions are aliased with each other.
- Resolution V: No main effect or two-factor interaction is aliased with any other main effect or two-factor interaction, but two-factor interactions are aliased with three-factor interactions.

Note: Avoid locking into a single type of DOE design. Learn from all sources! There are many methods in the DOE and no single method is best for all situations. Learn by taking the best from each method.

Inference Space

After we define our problem, we must make decisions about the limits of our study. The inference space of an experiment design represents how widely the results can be generalized beyond the samples used. It's the area within which conclusions (inferences) can be drawn, basically the span or focus of a study.

In a narrow-inference study, the experiment is focused on a specific subset of overall operation, such as only one shift, one operator, one machine, one batch, one line, etc. Narrow-inference studies are less affected by noise variables than broad-inference studies because the focus is narrowed. A broad-inference study usually addresses an entire process (all machines, all shifts, all operators, etc.), and generally more data must be taken over a longer time period. Broad-inference studies are affected by noise variables.

Step-by-Step Approach

The team must adopt a step-by-step approach to designing and conducting a DOE. It's essential for a cross-functional team to select the factors to study, design and conduct the experiment, analyze the data, make recommendations, and implement the results. It all requires careful planning and attention to detail to achieve success.

Don't assume that the more factors, the better the result. That's wrong! It's not the size of the DOE that's important, but the vital few factors you use in planning and what you do with the results.

> **Inference space** Extent to which one can draw conclusions (inferences) and generalize from the results of an experiment beyond the samples used, within the limits of the experiment design. **KEY TERM**

Let's refer to the Analyze phase and the major benefit that comes from doing Six Sigma DMAIC. In the Analyze phase, you verify the vital Xs to be included in the DOE in the Improve phase. If you jump into a DOE without sorting the vital few Xs, your experiment could be unmanageable. Why? Because the more factors you include, the larger and more complex your experiment and the longer it will take to perform the experiment; thus, you may do unnecessary DOEs.

For example, I did a DOE for Penn® tennis balls in a project to increase the bounce height of the ball. I did eight hypothesis tests of eight potential Xs, and we found two vital few Xs. This took two days, since the data was already in place in the parameter database within the process. I designed a two-factor experiment (DOE), which took an additional two days to get a final analysis and a setting to produce a 15.5% increase in bounce with only inline process setting. That's four days to complete a major breakthrough. Previous to using Six Sigma, the Penn internal quality group was doing a large-scale, nine-factor experiment called a Plackett-Burman design (highly complex with many errors). If they had done all combinations of the DOE with nine factors, they would have run 512 combinations to get the full view of all combinations (full resolution). They ran only 12 combinations of nine factors, which yielded nothing about the cause-and-effect relationship—and that result took three months.

Conducting the Experiment

As mentioned earlier, planning is the most important half of the DOE process; the analysis portion is straightforward and takes much less time. Conducting the experiment is simply a matter of following the plan—although simple doesn't necessarily mean easy or quick. That depends, of course, on your situation.

Project teams commonly make the error of not controlling the experiment. Operators/technicians may have the authority to change settings to prevent defects. You must explain why you're conducting the experiment and why you need the settings you've chosen—and that you're causing defects intentionally. Monitor the settings and provide reminders as necessary. Also monitor noise factors—shift, material, weather changes, or other possible sources of variation. Document all differences in the conditions.

Actively communicate your plan with all those concerned. This is vital to the success of an experiment.

To demonstrate DOE, let's walk through a break session we used at GE with a simple experiment.

Simple Example of Using Design of Experiments

Figure 7-9 shows an electromagnet made from a nail, a wire, and a battery. How many BB gun pellets can you lift? How much effect does each variable have on the lifting power? What's the cost of the best design?

1. Define the problem. Design a satisfactory electromagnet.

2. Establish the objective or hypothesis. Maximize the number of BBs picked up. Keep the costs in line.

3. Select the response variable(s), the Y(s). Number of BBs lifted.

4. Select the independent variable(s), the X(s). Build on facts learned during preliminary investigations.

Number of wire turns	Nail size
Number of batteries	Wire type
Battery arrangement	Nail head type

Experience shows that only two to six variables will be the vital few. The challenge is to identify the influential variables and find the test range that will illuminate these vital Xs. Test the most likely candidates first. Keep the design simple unless little is known and you need to test many variables to identify the most likely. It's a judgment call: Sometimes you'll be wrong. It's

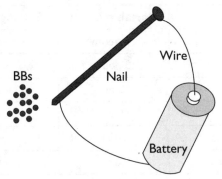

Figure 7-9. Nail-and-battery setup for electromagnet

not a failure when the experiment doesn't prove your hypothesis. It provides you with more information to move to the next experiment.

5. Choose the variable levels, the settings of the Xs to be studied. Build on facts learned during the preliminary investigations. You can use capability data to find the natural and extreme levels. Don't go beyond the safety level or physics of the problem. In initial experiments, usually two levels are used, different enough to detect effects. The two levels are designated as –1 (low) and +1 (high) (Figure 7-10).

Some combinations in the test will produce unacceptable results. That's to be expected.

Next we construct the array for the magnet experiment. We have three factors set at two levels. Therefore we will do a 2^3 (2 to the third) experiment: eight runs or treatment combinations. Figure 7-11 shows the design matrix with our treatment combinations.

> **POSITIVE ATTITUDE TOWARD EXPERIMENTS** FOR EXAMPLE
> It took more than 4,000 experiments to create the light bulb.
> "I have not failed. I've just found 10,000 ways that won't work." —Thomas A. Edison

Now we have another decision to make. Should we replicate the experiment? As you know from our earlier discussion, replications take more time and cost more, but they allow us to reduce variability and to better estimate error. For our example, we'll do one replication.

Variable	Variable Level	Setting Code
Nail	12 penny	– 1
Nail	20 penny	+1
Batteries	One	– 1
Batteries	Two	+1
Wire Turns	45	– 1
Wire Turns	35	+1

Figure 7-10. Three variables and their high (+1) and low (–1) settings

Run #	# Turns	# Batt	Nail Size
1	– 1	– 1	– 1
2	+1	– 1	– 1
3	– 1	+1	– 1
4	+1	+1	– 1
5	– 1	– 1	+1
6	+1	– 1	+1
7	– 1	+1	+1
8	+1	+1	+1

Figure 7-11. Design matrix of the treatment combinations

Running the Experiment

To this point the steps have taken us through all the planning activities covered in the first two thirds of this chapter. In the next step we put our plan into action.

6. Run the experiment and collect the data. If you've planned sufficiently and appropriately, running the experiment is straightforward. Here are some fundamental guidelines:

- Plan the DOE by anticipating potential problems with the trial.
- Adjust the test plan to minimize the effects of human error. "Human error" could be variations in such things as speed of picking up the BBs, placement of the nail amid the BBs, etc.

- Review the DOE plan with all the team members who will participate.
- Be physically present for the DOE to ensure it runs according to plan.
- Randomize the runs to reduce confounding and to spread out any variation due to run setup, different operators, noise factors (temperature, humidity, etc.), possible sequencing, and so on. However, there's the real-world issues of time and money. Do you have the resources to change all your factor settings after every run?
- Prepare the run sequence considering the following:
  - Difficulty of setup change;
  - Effect of time trends;
  - Changes of test equipment; and
  - Changes of ambient conditions.
- Prepare logical, clear data sheets to match the run sequence.
- Document conditions and any unplanned events.

Collecting the data is a critical step. It's said there's no such thing as a poor experiment, only one that's poorly designed or poorly executed. Poor planning leads to poor execution. It's vital that the people who'll run the DOE and set the factor levels understand the need for rigor and attention to detail throughout the experiment. One way to ensure this rigor and attention to detail is to do a dry run by verifying and improving the data-collection procedures before starting the experimental sequence.

The operators running the process are key to a successful experiment. Not only will they have to run the experiment in the planned sequence, but they will also need to record in detail any unusual occurrences during the experiment. They will need to reset the control variables, hold them constant, and usually measure the output from each experimental run.

I cannot overemphasize the need for highly capable measurement equipment, as the experiment's results can be greatly affected by measurement error. This common error can have serious consequences.

Setting controllable factor levels accurately is another key aspect of successful experimentation. The settings must be carefully monitored throughout the experiment.

Figure 7-12 shows the response data from of our electromagnet experiment. We can see that the treatment combinations used for runs 6

	A	B	C	Response
Run #	# Turns	# Batt	Nail Size	Bbs Lifted
1	– 1	– 1	– 1	14
2	+ 1	– 1	– 1	40
3	– 1	+ 1	– 1	21
4	+ 1	+ 1	– 1	38
5	– 1	– 1	– 1	34
6	+ 1	– 1	+ 1	136
7	– 1	+ 1	+ 1	4
8	+ 1	+ 1	+ 1	113

Figure 7-12. Response data from the electromagnet experiment

and 8 lifted the most BBs by far. We notice that the two treatment combinations differ only by the battery level. These results would suggest that the lower setting (one battery) gives better results than the high setting (two batteries), which surprises us.

Analyzing the Experiment Results

7. Analyze the data. The typical analysis will include a balanced ANOVA, main effect plots, interactive plots, a Pareto chart of effects, and percent contribution, at minimum.

To analyze the data from a DOE, the team must first evaluate the *statistical* significance. To do that, the team uses analysis of variance (ANOVA, explained in Chapter 6)—for a single factor, the *one-way ANOVA* or, for more than one factor, the *N-way ANOVA*.

The *practical* significance can be evaluated through the study of total sum of squares (your statistical software will handle this), pie charts, Pareto diagrams, main effects plots, and Normal probability plots. There are situations in which factors are statistically significant, but not practically significant. In any analysis, it's important to analyze every residual (the difference between a prediction and an observation) prior to drawing conclusions.

Figure 7-13 shows the ANOVA results for our electromagnet experiment.

Source	DF	SS	MS	F	P
N Turns	1	8064.5	8064.5	8.10	0.047
N Batteries	1	288.0	288.0	0.29	0.619
Nails, size	1	3784.5	3784.5	3.80	0.123
Error	4	3981.0	995.3		
Total	7	16,118.0			

Notes: DF = Degrees of freedom; SS = Sum of squares; MS = Mean square; F = F-statistic (between-group variation divided by within-group variation); P = p-value (probability of obtaining a test statistic result at least as extreme as the one actually observed, assuming that the null hypothesis is true); error = Unexplained variation.

Figure 7-13. ANOVA results for electromagnet experiment

Total sum of squares Quantity calculated as part of a standard way to present results of statistical data analyses, defined as the sum, overall observations, of the squared difference of each observation from the overall mean. Also known as sums **KEY TERMS** of squares.

Residual Difference between a prediction or expectation and an observation. The amount of variability in a dependent variable that remains after accounting for the variability explained by the predictors (independent variables) in data analysis.

The analysis (Figure 7-14) shows that the number of turns and the nail size are statistically significant and they matter from a practical standpoint. The number of batteries (one or two) has little effect on the number of BBs lifted.

The ANOVA table shows that all the effects are statistically significant at an alpha level of 0.05. P-values of less than 0.05 are statistically significant. The only one less than 0.05 is for the N-turns factor. Although the effects are all statistically significant, they aren't all practically significant, as demonstrated when we consider the magnitude of each sum-of-squares (SS) compared with the total sum-of-squares (Figure 7-14).

The percentage contribution of each factor indicates whether the factor is among the vital few. This may not matter much if you're testing

Factors	SS	% Contribution
N Turns	8064.5	50.0%
N Batteries	288.0	1.8%
Nails, size	3784.5	23.5%
Error	3981.0	24.7%
Total	16,118.0	

Figure 7-14. Table showing practical significance and percent contribution by each factor

only three factors, as in our electromagnet experiment. However, not identifying the right factors for DOE is a common mistake and can be costly, since it means spending more time and resources on further experimentation.

Error In statistical analysis, an unexplained variation in a collection of observations. DOEs typically require understanding both random error (occurs due to natural variation in the process) and lack-of-fit error (occurs when the analysis omits one or more important terms or factors from the process model).

KEY TERM

The number of turns was the most important factor, contributing 50.0% of the effects, and the number of batteries (one or two) was the least important factor, contributing only 1.8%. We see these results in terms of the effect of the factors on the BBs lifted in Figure 7-15.

We could also test for interactions in addition to main effects. In a real-life situation, it's important to evaluate whether and how much changing the settings of one factor affect another factor, because an interaction can

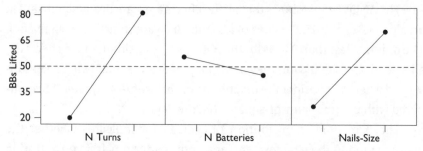

Figure 7-15. Main effects plot showing means for the BBs lifted

increase or decrease main
effects, sometimes a lot. As
mentioned earlier, that's a big
advantage of DOE over traditional, one-factor-at-a-time
experiments—DOE tests not
only for single-factor effects
(main effects) but also for
interactions between or among factors.

> **REPLICATE TO SEE
> SOURCES OF ERROR**
> Including replication in a DOE
> makes it possible to distin-
> guish between lack-of-fit
> error and random (pure) error and to
> estimate the random error.
>
> SMART
> MANAGING

If we tested for interactions of factors in our electromagnet experiment, our ANOVA would show the results for

N-Turns × N-Batteries

N-Turns × Nails-Size

N-Batteries × Nails-Size

Then we would create an interactions plot. On an interactions plot
(Figure 7-16), the plotted lines are parallel when there are no interactions
and nonparallel if there are interactions, with the degree of interaction
indicated by the difference in angle.

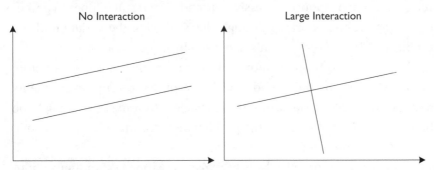

Figure 7-16. Interactions plot

The table in Figure 7-14 showing practical significance and percent
contribution by each factor shows the N-turns contribution calculation,
and you could use that table to explain the Error % calculation.

The Pareto chart (Figure 7-17) is a great way to illustrate the percent
contribution of each factor and the practical percentage of the cumulative effect of the Xs on the Y.

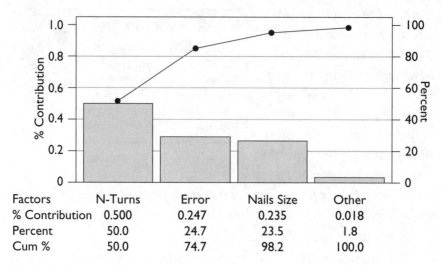

Factors	N-Turns	Error	Nails Size	Other
% Contribution	0.500	0.247	0.235	0.018
Percent	50.0	24.7	23.5	1.8
Cum %	50.0	74.7	98.2	100.0

Figure 7-17. Pareto chart showing results of electromagnet experiment

If you run balanced ANOVA—also known as ANOVA for balanced data—in Minitab, the test results will indicate excessive variation. Too much variation in the response is, of course, a function of the Xs in the process. You should have identified the Xs in the Analyze phase to reduce the variation in response. Excessive variation is a result of poor hypothesis testing and not working through the Xs driving the variation of the output Y. This is a common mistake made by project teams.

It's better and more economical to identify the vital few Xs before doing DOE, so you don't spend time and resources running experiments as a way to reduce the factors to those vital few. In some cases it might be better to reduce the scope of the problem to focus on one machine, one shift, one cell, one defect type, or whatever.

Another common mistake is to make the wrong assumptions about interactions among input variables. Because of lack of knowledge about the process or a poor design, a team may alias/confound the wrong factors or interactions or make an incorrect assumption of linearity. In either case, t may be surprised when the results of their experiment aren't what they expected and their model predicted.

Now that we've analyzed the data from our experiment, we can continue with the final two steps of the Design of Experiments process.

8. Draw conclusions. Once you've analyzed the data and determined the practical significance of each factor and interaction, you need to determine the combination of factors and interactions that optimizes the process to meet your critical objectives. It's good practice to replicate the optimum setup and ensure the results can be reproduced. When you've proved your findings, you draw conclusions and make recommendations to senior management.

If you're unable to find the optimum setting for a factor, it may be because you haven't experimented in the right ranges. This is a common mistake of project teams. It's also possible that the relationship between an X and a Y is linear for the settings for X used in the experiment, but nonlinear outside the range of those settings.

Check that you've considered all the observed data. Confine all initial conclusions and deductions to the experimental evidence. Make sure that you understand the meaning and business aspects of the DOE conclusion. The champion and the black belt need to discuss the results of the study and gain buy-in with the executives, depending on the changes needed. Always try to explain the analysis in both graphical and numerical terms to the process owners: A picture is worth a thousand numbers.

9. Achieve the objective. What if you find that you haven't optimized the process through your experiment? Apply what you've learned to plan the next DOE. It's impossible to fully optimize a process based on one experimental sequence.

When you've proved that the process is improved and is set at the optimum operating configuration, what comes next?

If you've reached this stage in your experimental process, then you're ready to institutionalize the changes, to ensure that entropy doesn't affect the optimized process over time. If we improve and optimize the process, but don't institutionalize the recommended changes and put controls on the key aspects of the process, the process will revert over time.

You're setting the stage for the Control phase to ensure the process will sustain the results. This is the main reason for the Control phase, using control techniques such as SPC to control the critical-to-process parameters, covered in the next chapter.

Review the Project with the Champion

The black belt meets with the champion to discuss the Improve phase of the project and to prepare for the phase-gate review that concludes the Improve phase. Here are some of the questions they may discuss:

- What solutions to the problem did the team consider?
- What criteria did the team use to decide on a solution?
- What solution did the team choose?
- How did the other solutions compare in terms of the criteria?
- How is the solution linked to the causes identified and verified in the Analyze phase?
- Did the results of the DOE surprise the team? If so, how?
- What setting level will be used to solve the problem? Is it the most economical?
- Were the results worth the cost of the DOE?
- What plans has the team developed to implement the solution?
- What new knowledge do we have as compared to not doing the DOE?

There are good, basic checklists and worksheets to help a team prepare for the phase-gate review in *The Six Sigma Way Team Fieldbook* by P. S. Pande et al., (McGraw-Hill, 2001).

Conduct an Improve Phase-Gate Review

The black belt holds a review at the end of the Improve phase and reports on the project status to the executive team. The phase-gate review gives the executive team members an opportunity to ask questions about the project, comment, discuss obstacles, allocate resources as necessary, ensure the project team is achieving the project goals according to schedule, and provide positive reinforcement to the project team. Phase-gate reviews are not technical; it's assumed that the master black belt and the black belt have worked out any technical issues. The review primarily ensures that the project is proceeding according to plan, the team is providing the deliverables by the milestones, and the project is on time and on budget.

Manager's Checklist for Chapter 7

☑ The team begins the Improve phase by selecting the product or process performance characteristics that it must improve to achieve the project goal.

☑ The team tests variables that have been filtered through the Analyze phase and identified as the vital few Xs. The objective is to form the $Y = f(X)$ relationships to be leveraged and to establish performance specifications.

☑ The team diagnoses the performance characteristics to reveal the major sources of variation, using correlation and regression analysis.

☑ Design of Experiments (DOE) is the main tool of the Improve phase. The team uses statistically designed experiments to identify the key process input variables (Xs).

☑ The purpose of the experiment is to make an informative event occur that can be observed. The DOE forces inputs to extreme levels and the output is recorded and analyzed.

☑ Designed experiments enable the team to identify the most influential factors associated with a particular CTQ characteristic, to define their relationships and understand interactions between and among various factors, and to get information to quickly improve the process.

☑ Other typical tools of the Improve phase include a balanced ANOVA (used to determine the percent contribution of each factor to the effects) and a main effects plot (to graphically demonstrate the influence of each factor on the output and the effects of the settings).

Control Phase

It is conceivable that some time man will have knowledge of all the laws of nature so that he can predict the future quality of product with absolute certainty.

— Walter A. Shewhart (1891-1967), the "father" of statistical process control

At this point the project team has gone through the Define, Measure, Analyze, and Improve phases of the six sigma DMAIC process. The black belt or green belt has identified the vital few Xs that have caused the defects and has defined the relationship for the CTQ or Y and the vital few Xs. Now the team must control the Xs that created the problem/defect to ensure a sustained Y or output. That's the sole purpose of the Control phase.

The Control phase is the hardest part of the DMAIC process. Why so hard? Because processes tend to slip back toward their original state. The control systems installed at the end must sustain the gain for both the financial and defect metrics established at the start of the project. Depending upon the defect, statistical process control (SPC) will be instituted to ensure a constant level of control is maintained. The controls must be robust enough to prevent process error and keep human nature from slipping back into the old ways. Robust in this case means that if something were to shift in the process within the normal conditions, the defect level would stay within limits to sustain the expected financial result.

The Control phase focus is to maintain the the transfer function equation—Y = f(X)—in order to sustain the improvements in the Ys. The team must:

- Evaluate and validate the solution.
- Assess the capability of the process within, between, and over time with respect to the sources of variation causing the problem.
- Establish control systems to ensure the solution works for the long term.
- Document and monitor the process using the metrics defined earlier in the project.
- Standardize procedures also known as standard work.
- Hand over the process to the process owners with training.
- Calculate the financial gains and document the entire project including plans going forward in a final report.

Control Phase Steps and Tools

Here are the basic steps or groups of activities of the Control phase:

- Check the results of the improvement.
- Update the FMEA for the process.
- Using the FMEA and Process map, build the control plan.
- Implement the control plans.
- Transition to the process owners.
- Monitor and install an audit process into the process.
- Close the project.

As you will learn, although the activities may follow this sequence, some will occur simultaneously and there may be some reiteration. Of course, the specifics will depend on the specific process, situation, organization, and people.

Below we list the essential tools of the Control phase that are covered in this chapter:

- Control plans
- Statistical process control
- Mistake proofing

Control Plan

The *control plan* is a management tool that ensures the performance improvements achieved by the team don't fade away after the team transfers the improved process back to the process owners. The plan must enable the process owners to control the process variables and sustain the capability and stability of the process over time. The control plan is one of the most important tools of the DMAIC process and a key element that differentiates Six Sigma projects from traditional projects.

A control plan provides a written description of the actions required to ensure that all process inputs and outputs will be in a state of control. The plan should include procedures for process setup, monitoring, control, and troubleshooting. The plans need to be complete enough to ensure that the process owners and operators can maintain over time the gains achieved by the Six Sigma project team.

Control plans are living documents, maintained and updated throughout the life cycle of a process. Updates are made as measurement and processing systems are improved. Control plans don't replace detailed operator instructions; they describe how the process will be controlled. The plans ensure that improvements are sustained and that a plan is in place for continuing to identify opportunities within the process. Control plans provide a written description of the actions that are required at each phase of the process to ensure that all process inputs and outputs will be in a state of control. Control plans are living documents maintained and updated throughout the lifecycle of a product. Updates are made as measurement and processing systems are improved.

Here are the steps for the control:

1. Indicate the appropriate category: Prototype, Pre-Launch, Production.
2. Show part name and description.
3. List primary contact responsible for the control plan.
4. Indicate ID number specified by customer.
5. Enter original date.
6. Enter date of last revision.
7. List of core team members.

8. Check ggage R&R legend.

9. Obtain customer approval (if required).

10. Assign the document number.

11. Document date of latest updates.

12. Indicate characteristic class and legend.

13. Create part/process number.

14. Describe process/operation.

15. Identify processing equipment.

16. List product characteristic (Y).

17. List process characteristic (X).

18. List numbers from FMEA.

19. List product specifications/tolerance.

20. List process specifications/tolerance.

21. List measurement technique.

22. List gauge number.

23. List R&R of measurement system.

24. List capability indices.

25. Document sampling plan.

26. Describe control method.

27. Describe reaction plan.

28. List name of division, plant, department.

29. Obtain necessary approvals.

Statistical Process Control

Statistical process control (SPC) is a statistically based graphing technique that uses control charts to monitor process variables. A *control chart* (or *Shewhart chart*) calculates upper and lower control limits from the normal variation of a stable process and plots a process statistic—such as a mean or a variance—against a sample number or time. If the data points cross either of the control limits indicating a shift in the process affecting the statistic of interest, the shift is detected and a reaction plan should be triggered.

SPC is similar to hypothesis testing. The *state of statistical control* (i.e., there is no uncontrolled or special-cause variation present) is considered the null hypothesis, and an out-of-control situation is the alternate hypothesis. Type I and type II errors (explained in Chapter 6) exist in control charts. A type I or alpha error occurs when a point falls outside the control limits even though no special cause is operating. A type II or beta error occurs if a special cause is missed because the chart is

> **Control chart** Times series graph with a center line representing the long-term expected average value of **KEY TERM** the specified process variable and two control limits, located at 3 sigma above and below the center line. In a stable process, 99.7% of all data points fall between the two control limits. Also known as *Shewhart chart.*

not sensitive enough to detect it. In this case the SPC is a continuous on-going hypothesis over time constantly comparing present to past performance real-time.

Control performance is measured by average run length statistics. The *average run length* of a control chart is defined as the average number of samples taken between signals that a one-sigma shift has been detected. Control charts help us detect out-of-control processes; they don't explain why the process is out of control. However, attentive use of control charts can help us identify assignable causes for problems.

Figure 8-1 shows a basic control chart.

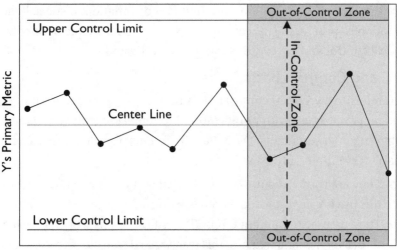

Figure 8-1. Basic control chart anatomy

By default:

- The center line is at the average of the specified process variable.
- The upper control limit is 3 sigma above the center line.
- The lower control limit is 3 sigma below the center line.

Special causes result in variation that can be detected, explained, and controlled. Examples include differences in supplier, material batch, new equipment, new shift, or something that happends on a particular day of the week. Variation from common causes, on the other hand, is inherent in the process. A process is in control when the process output is affected only by common causes—not by special causes. In other works, a process is in control when the data points fall within the bounds of the control limits and the points don't display nonrandom patterns.

We should reiterate here the distinction between the two types of variation. *Controlled variation*, or *common-cause variation*, occurs naturally and is inherent and expected in a stable process. This type of variation can be attributed to chance or random causes. *Uncontrolled variation*, or *special-cause variation*, occurs when an abnormal action enters a process and produces unexpected and unpredictable results. These sources of variability that are not part of the chance-cause pattern are considered *assignable* causes. Abnormal, unexpected, unusual indications of these causes may appear as nonrandom (patterned) variation. If special-cause variation is present, the process metric is said to be unstable or out of statistical control and the causes should be investigated.

SPC and Control Charts

SPC refers to a group of control charts that display process input or output data over time—with points plotted to represent statistical values of subgroup measurements (X, X-bar, R, S, etc.) through time. Control charts serve three purposes:

1. They are used to control the CTP (critical-to-process) characteristic; this use is called statistical process control.
2. They are used to monitor CTQ, CTC (critical-to-cost), or CTD (critical-to-delivery) characteristics; this use is called statistical process monitoring (*SPM*; discussed below).
3. They are used as diagnostic tools for any CT (critical-to) characteristics.

The data on control charts form patterns that can be statistically tested and, as a result, lead to information about the behavior of product and/or process characteristics. To evaluate this behavior, we use historical statistics of the process such as the mean and the standard deviations, statistical control limits, and different tests of out-of-control situations. Control charts enable the project team to detect assignable causes that affect the *central tendency* (a central value or a typical value for a probability distribution) and/or the variability of the cause system and identify when action is needed on the process. To sustain the use of SPC, the charts must be reviewed, changes must be made as indicated (such as adjusting the sampling interval, combining charts, and eliminating charts found unnecessary), and the team or the process owners must act on the information provided by the charts.

> **Central tendency** Central value or typical value for the probability distribution of a data set. The most **KEY TERM** common measures of central tendency are the *arithmetic mean* (average), the *median* (middle value when the number of values is odd, average of the two middle values when the number of values is even), and the *mode* (most frequently occurring value).

Basic Components of a Control Chart

As shown in the basic control chart (Figure 8-1), the vertical axis represents the scale of statistics associated with the CT characteristic and the horizontal axis represents the numbers of the subgroup samples in chronological order.

Each subgroup is characterized by its conditional distribution, which corresponds to the short-term variation (i.e., within-subgroup variation). Each subgroup statistic (e.g., mean, range, and standard deviation) is represented by a dot on the chart; these points form a marginal distribution (i.e., between-subgroup variation). It's customary to connect the sample points on the control chart with straight-line segments, to make it easier to visualize how the sequence of points evolves over time.

As shown in Figure 8-1, the center line, running through the control chart horizontally, represents the average of subgroup statistical values for the process. The center line is always the average of the plotted points on a control chart, regardless of the statistic plotted.

...e two more horizontal lines, conventionally three standard ...us or (±3σ) above and below the center line—the upper control ...mit (UCL) and the lower control limit (LCL). The UCL and LCL are set so that if the process is in control, 99.7% of the data points fall between them.

> **KEY TERM**
>
> **Control limit** Either of two lines drawn horizontally on a control chart, one (upper control limit, UCL) 3 sigma above the center line and the other (lower control limit or LCL) 3 sigma below the center line. If the process is in control, 99.7% of the data points will fall between the control limits, a zone that represents random, common-cause variation.

The control limits define three major zones (see Figure 8-1). The zone between the control limits represents random variation; the two zones below and above the control limits represent nonrandom variation. With the control limits, we can judge the variation of a CT characteristic. We consider a CT characteristic to be in control when all points fall inside the control limits and display only random variation, i.e., no specific patterns.

Figure 8-2 shows a control chart with the UCL and LCL established for the plotted and projected data points. Superimposed on the right, for comparison, is the ideal distribution curve—normal and fitting completely within the control limits.

When we create a control chart, we must have at least 20 initial points to calculate the *trial control limits*. These limits allow us to determine whether the process was in control when the initial samples were selected. If all points fall within the control limits and no systematic behavior is evident, then we conclude that the process was in control and the trial control limits are suitable for controlling current and future performance.

Once the control limits are established, they are maintained for any future samples taken from the same process and run under the same conditions. The limits are essential for evaluating whether the process remains in control and stable. As long as the new point plots are within the control limits, the process is assumed to be in control and no action is necessary. Since these control limits make it possible to distinguish between common-cause (intrinsic) variation and special-cause variation, they should keep us from reacting to expected variation.

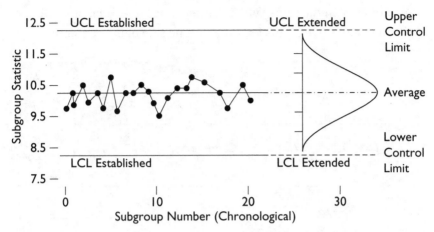

Figure 8-2. Sample control chart with superimposed distribution curve

Generally, the effective use of any control chart requires periodic revision of the control limits and center lines. Some practitioners set regular periodic reviews and revisions of control chart limits, such as every week, every month, or every 25, 50, or 100 samples.

Out of Control

When a process produces a normal distribution and is stable and under control, only 0.135% of the data points are beyond the control limits, so we expect points to plot within this zone and to be distributed randomly. However, if a process is out of control, the control chart shows points outside the control limits and/or distributed systematically, in patterns. An out-of-control condition indicates that process behavior has changed significantly, so it should be investigated and corrective action taken.

There are several types of patterns that indicate a process is out of control such as cycles, shifts, trends, etc. One set of guidelines is to be found in the original Western Electric handbook, *Statistical Quality Control*. These rules are based on industrial experience and have been observed to work for most processes. They also have a basis in probability theory.

- At least one point is outside the 3-sigma control limits.
- Two of three consecutive points are more than 2 sigma away from the center line, on the same side (in zones A or F, Figure 8-3).
- Four of five consecutive points are more than 1 sigma away from the

center line, on the same side (in either zones B or E, Figure 8-3).

■ Eight consecutive points are on the same side of the center line.

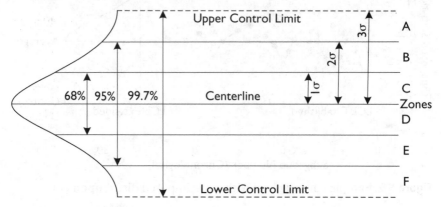

Figure 8-3. Control chart showing zones for interpreting Western Electric rules

Behavior of Processes

The behavior of a process is a manifestation of random variation, due only to white noise, and special cause variation to which we can assign an identifiable cause, also called black noise. *White noise* is mainly due to the level of technology in the process and is related to *process entitlement*—the level of performance a process should be able to achieve. *Black noise* is the main object of Six Sigma improvements; we must eliminate it so our processes can achieve six-sigma performance.

The five process conditions represented in Figure 8-4 exhibit different problems with centering and/or variation. However, in all cases we should strive to decrease the standard deviation and to center the mean on the target value. This is the overriding goal!

To sustain the improvements, SPC must enable us to control both process centering and process spread. Control charts show the operator whether the process is behaving "normally" (showing ran-

White noise In statistical process control, random or "natural" variation, intrinsic in a process, due to common causes.

KEY TERMS

Black noise Nonrandom variation, extrinsic to a process, due to special causes.

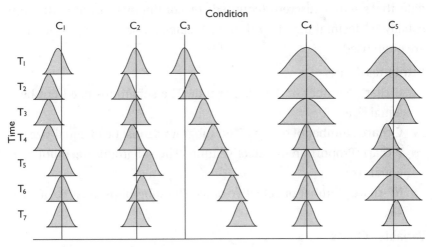

Figure 8-4. Process behaviors

dom variation only) or exhibiting variation due to special causes.

Implementing Control Charts

In implementing control charts, the team should consider such issues as availability of resources (money, people, etc.), time constraints, risk and confidence requirements, impact on specific parties, potential benefits to be derived, and potential for successful implementation.

The six-step approach for implementing control charts is as follows:

1. Define the problem.
2. Establish the measurement system.
3. Determine which control charts to use.
4. Prepare to collect process data.
5. Implement the control charts.
6. Use the control charts and improve the process continuously.

When selecting control charts, the team should consider criteria such as the sample size, the desired sensitivity level for detecting small shifts in the process, and the allowable complexity level of the charts.

Types of Charts

As mentioned in Chapter 6, statisticians distinguish between *attributes data*—data that fit into categories that can be described in terms of words (attributes), such as good/bad or pass/fail, and *variables data,*

data that's either discrete (counted) or continuous (on a continuum, usually in decimal form). Within each category several types of charts are often used.

Attributes Charts

- **U chart.** Number of defects per unit. The subgroups need not be of equal size.
- **C chart.** Number of defects. The subgroups must be of equal size.
- **P-chart.** Proportion of defective units. The subgroups need not be of equal size.
- **NP-chart.** Number of defective units. The subgroups must be of equal size.

Variables Charts

- **X_i–MR chart (individuals and moving range chart).** Used to track both X and Y. It consists of two separate charts: The individuals chart tracks individual measurements; the moving range chart tracks the range between one individual measurement and the next.
- **X-bar–R chart (average and range chart).** Used to track X and/or Y. It consists of two separate charts: The average chart tracks the subgroup average; the range chart tracks the range within each subgroup.
- **X-bar–S chart (average and sigma chart).** Used when you can rationally collect measurements in subgroups, so each subgroup represents a "snapshot" of the process at any one point in time. It consists of two separate charts: the average chart tracks the average of values for each period; the sigma chart tracks the standard deviation of the values for the period.
- **Pre-control chart.** Used mainly during setup to make run/no-run decisions on the production line. The output, Y, is the variable of interest.
- **EWMA chart (exponentially weighted moving average chart).** Used to monitor both X and Y and to detect small shifts and drifts in the process. EWMA averages data samples in a way that weights the most recent samples most heavily and gives progressively less weight to earlier samples.

The control chart possibilities may seem overwhelming. The control chart road map (Figure 8-5) should help you decide which charts to use for the data you want to track.

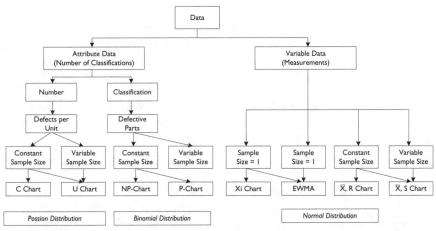

Figure 8-5. Control chart road map

Poisson distribution Probability distribution that characterizes discrete events occurring independent of one another in time.

KEY TERM

Binomial distribution Probability distribution for the number of times an outcome with a constant probability will occur in a succession of repetitions of a statistical experiment.

Using Control Charts

Here are the basic steps for using control charts:

1. Select the appropriate variable to chart. Ideally this should be a critical X.
2. Select the type of control chart to use.
3. Determine rational subgroup size and sampling interval/frequency.
4. Determine measurement method and criteria.
5. Do a gauge (sometimes spelled gage) capability study, if necessary (Figure 8-6).
6. Calculate the parameters of the control chart.
7. Gather the data.

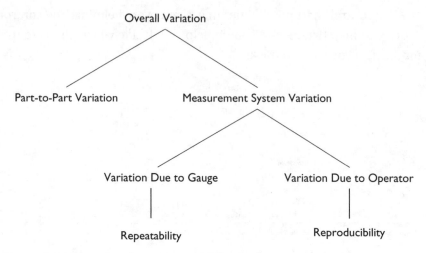

Figure 8-6. Example of gauge capability study

8. Calculate the control limits.
9. Train the necessary people.
12. Implement and analyze the charts.The following pages describe two
    control charts, the P-chart and the X-bar chart, and explain how they
    are used.

P-Chart

The *p-chart* is widely used for attributes data. The purpose is to observe
and evaluate the behavior of a process over time and against control limits and to take corrective action if necessary. Figure 8-7 shows an example.

The p-chart plots the proportion of defective units collected from subgroups of equal or unequal size. The *p* stands for *proportion* of defective
units in a subgroup. (P-charts differ from np-charts in that they plot the
proportion of defective units, rather than the *number* of defective units.)

Major Considerations for P-Charts

The p-chart plots the proportion of defective units, not the proportion of
defects. A p-chart is preferred over an np-chart if using the rate of defective units is more meaningful than using the actual number of defective
units and if the subgroup or sample size varies from period to period.

Large subgroup sizes should always be selected (n > 50 is considered
normal) and the np value should always be greater than 5.

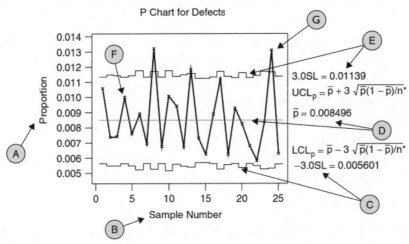

Figure 8-7. P-Chart (Source: *Statistical Process Control (SPC) Reference Manual*, pp. 91–110)

Terminology:

(A) Proportion = Number of defective units observed in the sample divided by the number of units sampled

(B) Sample number = Chronological index number for the sample or subgroup whose proportion of defective units is being referenced

(C) and (E) Lower control limit (LCL), Upper control limit (UCL) = Since the sample size varies, the control limits are recalculated each time, resulting in a "staircase" effect

(D) P-Bar = Average value of the proportion of defective units in each subgroup over the period of inspection

(F) In control, random data point.

(G) Any point in this plot above the UCL or below the LCL represents an out-of-control condition to be investigated

Application

1. Determine the purpose of the chart.
2. Select the data-collection point.
3. Establish the basis for subgrouping.
4. Establish the sampling interval and determine the sample size.
5. Set up forms for recording and charting data. Write specific instructions on use of the chart.
6. Collect and record data. It is recommended that at least 20 samples be used to calculate the control limits.

7. Compute p, the proportion nonconforming for each of the i sub-groups.
8. Compute the process average proportion nonconforming p, which is the average value of the proportion of defective units in each subgroup over the period of inspection being referenced.
9. Compute the upper control limit, UCL_p.
10. Compute the lower control limit, LCL_p.
11. Plot the data points.
12. Interpret the chart, together with other pertinent sources of information on the process. Take corrective action if necessary.

X-Bar Chart

The X-bar chart (Figure 8-8) is widely used for variables data. *X-bar* refers to the sample average value (X) being plotted. (An X with a bar over it is the standard statistical symbol for "mean of all X values.") The *X-bar chart* plots the average values of each of a number of small sampled subgroups. The X-bar chart is usually plotted in conjunction with the R (range) chart or the S (standard deviation) chart.

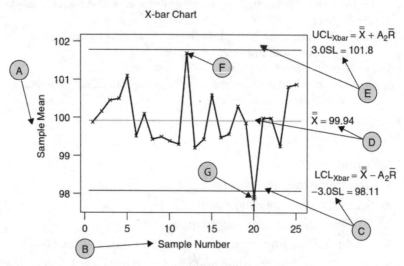

X-bar Chart

Terminology
(A) Sample mean = Means of the process subgroups as collected in sequential or chronological order
(B) Sample number = Chronological index number for the sample or subgroup whose average value is being referenced

(C) Lower control limit (LCL)

(D) Process average = Overall average value of the individual process readings, over the period of inspection

(E) Upper control limit (UCL)

(F) A point near the control limit

(G) Any point in this plot above the UCL or below the LCL represents an out-of-control condition to be investigated

Figure 8-8. X-bar chart (Source: *Statistical Process Control Reference Manual*, pp. 29–68)

Minitab has a number of tests available for out-of-control conditions. It labels each point with a number corresponding to the test that shows where the particular output represented by the point failed to pass.

Major Considerations for X-Bar Charts

The X-bar chart, together with the R chart, is a sensitive control chart for identifying assignable causes of product and process variation and provides insight into short-term variations. The control limits for the X-bar chart differ, depending on whether it's being plotted for use with the R chart or with the S chart.

Application

1. Determine the purpose of the chart.
2. Select the data-collection point.
3. Establish the basis for subgrouping.
4. Establish the sampling interval and determine sample size equal to n.
5. Set up forms for recording and charting data. Write specific instructions on use of the chart.
6. Collect and record data. A minimum of 25 subgroups or samples of size equal to n should be measured.
7. Compute the process average, referred to as X-bar or X.
8. If using the R chart, compute the average moving range R. If using the S chart, compute the average standard deviation S.
9. Compute the upper control limit, $UCL_{X\text{-bar}}$.
10. Compute the lower control limit, $LCL_{X\text{-bar}}$.
11. Plot the data points.
12. Interpret the chart, together with other pertinent sources of information on the process. Take corrective action if necessary.

Control Charts

Control charts are the application tools of SPC. Remember that SPC (statistical process control) is a set of statistical methods used to assess and achieve process stability and capability. Please take note that SPC is simply an ongoing test comparing current with historical data to constantly monitor and ensure *process capability*.

■ With Six Sigma, control charts for continuous data are used to control critical-to-process (CTP) characteristics; monitor critical-to-quality (CTQ), critical-to-cost (CTC), and critical-to-delivery (CTD) characteristics; or diagnose any CT characteristics.

■ Control charts enable us to simultaneously control process centering and variation.

■ Control charts are a practical tool for detecting changes in product and/or process performance.

■ The control limits are essential to evaluate whether the process remains in control and stable.

■ The control limits are set at a distance of plus or minus three standard deviations of the center line ($\pm 3\sigma$). At least 20 points must be used to calculate the control limits.

■ The zone between the control limits represents random variation; the zone outside the limits is the area of nonrandom variation.

■ Out-of-control conditions such as cycles, shifts, trends, and stratification send a clear message that process behavior has changed, so bshould be investigated and corrective action taken.

■ The principal types of control charts for continuous data used in Six Sigma are X-MR, X-bar-R, X-bar-S, and EWMA. X-bar-R charts are powerful tools and the most commonly used.

■ The success of control charts depends on the proper selection of subgroups.

Contingency Plans for Out-of-Control Conditions

What happens if process measures indicate an out-of-control condition? The project team should plan for that possibility by developing, communicating, explaining, and deploying response plans. The basis for good contingency plans is any FMEA conducted during the earlier phases of the project. The results show the potential problems, the likely effects, and the best ways to handle each problem.

The team should establish the critical parameters to monitor. That may be all the variables for which there are control charts, or it may be selected variables. The response plan should include instructions on specific corrective actions to take when identified factors cause the process to go out of control. If possible, it should also include a troubleshooting guide.

Minimizing the Potential for Problems—Mistake Proofing

We can minimize the potential for problems through mistake proofing (aka error proofing or *poka-yoke*, the original Japanese term). This concept of using experience, wisdom, and ingenuity to remove opportunities for errors in activities and processes is consistent with the goals and philosophy of Six Sigma and widely applied in a broad range of processes.

The methodology involves understanding cause-and-effect relationships and identifying the simplest remedies that can help eliminate future errors. For example:

- A stop is added to a drill press.
- A hydraulic ram is added to an assembly process to help operators align a component.
- A pin is added so that assemblers cannot install a part backward.
- Fields on a data entry form are highlighted as being critical.
- An authorization procedure is introduced to control spending.
- A checklist is created to ensure that people planning a training session don't overlook essential items.
- A policy is developed to ensure that employees complete expense claims properly.

Often, mistake proofing focuses on errors produced by humans, whether it's the machine operator, the person filling out a form, someone packing materials, and so on. The emphasis should be on modifying processes so people won't make mistakes, instead of blaming employees for mistakes.

The mistake-proofing planning sheet (Figure 8-9) provides an organized, logical tool for reducing the opportunities for error.

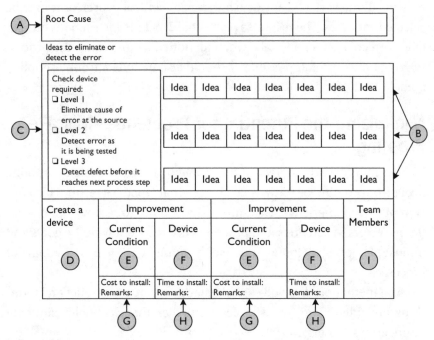

Figure 8-9. Mistake-proofing planning sheet (Source: *Quality Planning and Analysis: From Product Development Through Use*, p. 347)

1. Identify the root cause of the error or defect (A).
2. For each step in the problematic process, brainstorm and list ideas for ways to eliminate the problem (B).
3. Indicate where in the process the defect or error should be detected or prevented—before it occurs, as it is occurring, or after it has occurred (C).
4. Describe for each problem condition (E) the improvements, devices, or methods for eliminating the defect or error (D and F).
5. Give the cost of implementing the improvement and the length of time needed to install it (G and H).
6. Identify the team members involved in developing and implementing the mistake-proofing plan (I).

Mistake Proofing: Recap

Mistake proofing is a methodology for avoiding mistakes in a process. It can work when other, more analytical methods can't be applied or don't produce results. The technique involves the use of experience, wisdom, and ingenuity to create devices that will reduce opportunities for errors. Since mistake proofing applies in such a wide range of areas, it's possible only to provide general guidelines: There are no rules or structure that fit all situations.

There are several levels of control for mistake proofing. It may only be possible to detect a mistake and issue a warning, or it may be possible to eliminate the possibility of making the mistake. Obviously, whenever possible, prevention is better than detection.

Mistake proofing does not apply only to human error; it can be applied to automated machines, computer software, or any process that contains variation. It's the primary means of control for transactional processes through standard operating procedures, forms, checklists, etc. Mistake proofing is applied in the engineering environment by the use of FMEAs that document all possible failure modes of every component and system associated with the product.

Examples of mistake proofing are all around us. We may not even realize how many products and services have been designed help us avoid mistakes.

Plan for Transfer to Process Owners

After the project team completes the Six Sigma project, it needs to transfer the improved process to the process owners and operators. This requires documenting the process, communicating the improvements and benefits, training the owners and operators to assume their new responsibilities to monitor the process performance, and institutionalizing the changes.

The project team must develop a transition plan so process owners and operators can understand how the process has been changed and what those changes mean in terms of their responsibilities.

- How will the responsibilities for monitoring the process be transferred from the improvement team to the process owner?

- How will the process owner verify improvement in present and future process capabilities and sigma levels?
- What's the recommended audit plan for routine surveillance inspections of the project's gains?
- What's the recommended auditing frequency?
- What control charts and other quality tools will the process owner need to use?

We need to stress two points. One is the reality behind the sigma shift: Process performance naturally tends to decline over the long term. The other point is expressed in this anonymous quote:

> It's not a single, great, heroic deed that defines who you really are. It's the little things you do day by day that count.

Problems can arise if the transfer plan isn't properly developed and implemented. The process owners may be willing to accept the process improvement, but not their new responsibilities for documenting and monitoring the process according to the control plan. Consequently, the problem returns. The transfer plan and the control plan should establish some means of ensuring that the process owners are accountable for the new level of process performance in the long term.

It's often easier to change a process than to change the people who are responsible for operating that process and sustaining the gains. That's why institutionalization is critical to Six Sigma—and why it's as much about psychology as about processes.

Effective documentation requires some of the same wisdom and ingenuity as mistake proofing: How can you counter any reasons that the owners and operators might have for not accepting and supporting the process improvements?

The black belt, the champion, and the master black belt should develop a training plan for the process owners and operators. The training should include instructions for reading and interpreting control charts, guidance in understanding and using all the documentation on the improved process, and knowing the contingency response plan and how to implement it if necessary. Training should also include an understanding of how the process was improved and the financial and other benefits of the improvement.

Essential to instituting the improvement is for the team to develop standards and procedures and to document and communicate them to all stakeholders, particularly to the owners and operators of the process.

The documentation should include:

- A detailed description of the process to be controlled;
- Detailed maps of the improved process;
- Updated operating procedures—for both routine and unusual situations;
- A list of all variables to be measured and controlled;
- A description of methods, techniques, and tools to be used to obtain data;
- Instructions for monitoring the process, analyzing the data, and interpreting the control charts;
- Checklists; and
- Flowcharts.

All this documentation should be developed to make it easy for the process owners and operators to understand and to use. The language should be simple and clear. Use short sentences. Illustrate with flowcharts. Provide checklists.

The project team must document the new responsibilities of the process owner and operators, the new SOP and standards, and the quality tools to monitor the process and ensure the process gains will be sustained.

The champion and members of the executive team, in consultation with the master black belt, are responsible for documenting the lessons learned. Each Six Sigma project will add to what the organization knows about its processes and the methodology for improving them—but that knowledge will be power only if it's shared throughout the organization through documentation, institutionalization, and training. This is an important part of change management, essential for transforming and maintaining an organizational culture that embraces change and improvement.

The project team should ensure that its improvements are institutionalized—that all new process steps, standards, and documentation are integrated into normal operations and that systems, procedures, policies, instructions, and budgets are modified to sustain the gains achieved through Six Sigma.

Communication Plans

Communication in the Control phase should cover four purposes:

1. Describe and explain the improvements and the new process—for the process owners and operators.
2. Summarize the project and share all lessons learned—for other current and future champions and black belts as well as for anybody responsible for training.
3. List for management the improvements and report on all the benefits achieved and expected—particularly financial.
4. Spread the word about Six Sigma and the success achieved on this project—for the entire organization.

The first type of communication was outlined above in the discussion of documentation. It's part of the control plan, essential to transferring the process back to the owners.

The second type of communication—project summary and lessons learned—should be almost complete at this point. The project team has been documenting its activities from the start of the project and reporting on its findings at the phase-gate reviews that end each phase of the DMAIC model. Responsibility for drafting a report from the documentation maintained throughout the project could be delegated to members of the team, by phases. The black belt and the champion can then compile the reports for each phase and finalize the full report.

This report should be a comprehensive statement of what the team did and what it learned from the project. It should state each project objective and outline the steps taken in each phase toward the objectives. It should indicate where the team found defects and problems, what statistical tools it used to identify them, what corrective actions the black belt decided to take and the reasons for that decision, and the results of the action.

Each project report becomes part of the knowledge base accessible to the executive team and Six Sigma for future projects. They show how a team has proceeded, explain why, and describe the results. The champion must make sure that all lessons learned are entered into whatever system the executive team has set up for documenting and sharing Six Sigma knowledge.

The third type of communication—reporting on the benefits, particularly financial, to management—should be relatively easy, since that's been the focus of the project from the outset, when the executive team listed and prioritized potential projects. It's even easier if the team has worked with a representative of the financial department in the Define phase, at least. At this point, the black belt and the champion should have all the facts and figures they need to prepare a report on the benefits of the project.

The second and third types of communication may be combined, depending on the organization and the means of reporting and disseminating information. If the black belt and the champion prepare a report that will summarize the project, share lessons learned, and present the benefits of the project, here's some guidance.

To be effective, final reports need to include certain key elements that present and quantify a given project's objectives. While each one is unique to the problem addressed, there are seven basic sections that need to be included in each report. Within each section, you can be as specific as necessary about a given project in terms of how you measured, analyzed, improved, and controlled the problem. Here are the seven main sections and their subsections that you need to develop:

1. Executive Summary (main problem, project goals, project results)
   Problem Statement
   Customer Requirements
   Project Objectives
   Outline of Project Strategy
   Project Schedule
   Final Project Description

2. Experimental Data (actions taken)
   Gauge Studies
   Materials Characterization (if appropriate)
   Process Specifications
   Capability Studies (short- and long-term)
   Design of Experiments

3. Implementation
   Operating Specification

Process FMEA

Performance Tracking Systems

Performance Data

Support Systems

Control Plans

4. Conclusions

Discussion of Results

Lessons Learned/Recommendations

List of Project Team Members

Data Storage

Every Six Sigma improvement project is different. The final report must address the unique concerns and conclusions of the specific problem. It may also include suggestions or recommendations for future Six Sigma projects.

This outline of main headings is a only a guide to understanding the basics of a final report. As you conduct each project, you can include the critical information that you and the project team have gathered to justify the project goals and demonstrate how and why you reached your conclusions.

Finally, the fourth type of communication—spread the word about Six Sigma and the success achieved on this project to the entire organization—began when the team was formed and will continue indefinitely in various ways. When people are doing something that promises to provide significant returns, they tend to talk about it. When people are learning, when they're confronting challenges and resolving problems, they tend to talk about it.

The project champion should encourage the team members to share their experiences with their coworkers. The champion should take advantage of any opportunities to discuss the project and Six Sigma. This is especially important when the organization is beginning its Six Sigma initiative because successful projects should convince the skeptics and even make enthusiastic advocates of at least some of them. They can't easily or logically argue with the financial results. As the saying goes, "Money talks and BS walks."

Talk about what you and the team have done and what you've

accomplished. Emphasize what it could mean to the rest of the organiza-tion. What did you and the team learn that could help others? What knowledge could be leveraged elsewhere? What other areas of the organ-ization might benefit from the ongoing improvements and the lessons learned? Because they're your colleagues, other managers may be inter-ested in what you've done—but they'll pay better attention if they know there are benefits in it for them.

Promote your project, promote the system through which project knowledge and lessons learned can be shared, and promote Six Sigma.

Review the Project with the Champion

The black belt meets with the champion to discuss the Control phase of the project, to prepare for the phase-gate review that will conclude this phase and this Six Sigma project. Here are some questions they may dis-cuss:

- Did the solution achieve the project objectives?
- What are the vital few Xs? What key inputs and outputs will be meas-ured and monitored ongoing?
- What's the plan for monitoring and controlling the inputs and out-puts? How will the process owners and operators sustain the gains and detect out-of-control conditions?
- Which control charts will be used? How will the control charts be checked and interpreted to monitor performance?
- What's the plan for training the process owners and operators?
- How has the team documented the improvements and the new process?
- What mistake-proofing ideas have been implemented in the process?
- Are there other areas of the organization where the improvements could be replicated? If so, how?
- What lessons has the team learned about Six Sigma and structures and dynamics vis-à-vis the organization that could benefit other Six Sigma teams?
- Are the black belt and the champion ready for the project sign-off?

There are good, basic checklists and worksheets to help a team pre-pare for the phase-gate review in *The Six Sigma Way Team Fieldbook*.

Conduct a Control Phase-Gate Review

The black belt and the champion hold a review at the end of the Control phase in which they report to the executive team on the project's status. The review gives the executive team an opportunity to ask questions about the project and reports.

At this final phase-gate review, the black belt and the champion finalize the project with a sign-off with the controller, after a financial audit, and with the appropriate managers, as a formality of turning over ownership of the improved process.

Recognize and Celebrate

As mentioned earlier, the fourth type of communication in the communication plan is to spread the word about Six Sigma and the success achieved on this project to the entire organization. The project champion publicizes the results and recognizes the work done by the team members.

Of course, if your organization has a system for rewarding members of Six Sigma teams for their contributions, as we strongly recommended in Chapter 2, make sure the team members are not only recognized but also rewarded. But whether the team members share a little in the financial benefits they've achieved or not, the champion should do whatever possible to make sure they receive some recognition for their work.

When the project is officially ended and the paperwork completed, it's time to celebrate the project, an important part of the Six Sigma culture. When you celebrate a completed project, it's not only recognition of the success and financial benefits, but also recognition of the teamwork, the enthusiasm, and the persistence that went into that success.

Control Phase Deliverables

The basic deliverables for the Control phase include:

- Project status form/timeline;
- Statement of practical solutions;
- Cost-benefit analysis of potential solutions;
- Justification of selected solutions;
- Verification of improvement results (metrics and savings);

- Implementation plan for solutions;
- Control plan, including the:
  - training plan;
  - documentation plan;
  - monitoring plan;
  - response plan;
  - institutionalization plan to align systems and structures;
- Implementation of solutions and control plan;
- Capability analysis;
- Project summary and lessons learned;
- Final report; and
- Phase-gate review and sign-off, including verification of financial impact and transfer of ownership (project closure).

Summary

In the Control phase, the team works to maintain the changes that it made in the Xs as so to sustain the improvements in the Ys. The team must first develop a control plan, consisting of five parts: training plan, documentation plan, monitoring plan, response plan, and institutionalization plan.

With the training plan, the black belt, the champion, and the master black belt develop a training plan for the process owners and operators. The plan should include instructions for reading and interpreting control charts, understanding and using all the documentation on the improved process, and the contingency response plan and how to implement it.

With the documentation plan, the project team should ensure that its improvements are institutionalized—that all new process steps, standards, and documentation are integrated into normal operations and that systems, procedures, policies, instructions, and budgets are modified to sustain the gains achieved.

With the monitoring plan, the team must document and monitor the process using the metrics defined earlier in DMAIC, evaluate the solution, assess the process capability over time, and establish control systems to ensure the solution works for the long term.

With the response plan, the team must establish the checkpoints that would signal out-of-control conditions and define the actions to be taken.

With the institutionalization plan, the team tries to align systems and structures to ensure the changes will continue. The team develops standards and procedures, and it documents and communicates them to all stakeholders, particularly to the process owners and operators.

Finally, the team members and the controller calculate, verify, and document the project's financial gains. At that point, the black belt and the champion close the Control phase and formally end the project with the final phase-gate review, handing over the process to the process owners. Last, the team celebrates its success and the teamwork that made it possible.

Manager's Checklist for Chapter 8

☑ The purpose of the Control phase is solely to control the Xs to ensure a sustained Y.

☑ The goal of the Control phase is to use process data to monitor the process and adjust it as necessary to make it perform as intended.

☑ The Control phase is usually initiated by selecting those product or process performance characteristics that must be improved to achieve the goal.

☑ The control plan is the central tool of the DMAIC process, one of the important elements that differentiates Six Sigma projects from traditional improvement projects.

☑ Mistake proofing is the use of experience, wisdom, and ingenuity to remove or reduce opportunities for errors.

☑ Statistical process control (SPC) must be installed to sustain a constant level of improved performance.

☑ SPC is an ongoing in-process hypothesis test, a statistically based graphing technique that compares current process data with a set of stable control limits. Those control limits are statistically based on normal process variation and enable the detection of shifts in the process of the critical statistic of interest (e.g., mean, variance, etc.)

How to Sustain
Six Sigma

The best Six Sigma projects begin not inside the business but outside it, focused on answering the question, how can we make the customer more competitive?

—Jack Welch, former CEO,
General Electric

Making your customers more competitive is a key sign that you're successfully implementing Six Sigma. If your performance meets or exceeds the customers' expectations for quality, delivery, and cost, then all your hard work in problem-solving projects has achieved its objective. But is that where it ends?

Of course not. You don't make the investment in Six Sigma and take the time to train people, to select projects, and then to drill down to your costs of poor quality *once*. Six Sigma is ongoing; it's a constant, "living" methodology that needs to continue as long as your business does.

Naturally, individual projects that fix specific problems have start and finish dates, but as part of your Six Sigma commitment, you need to initiate new projects, find more dollars, raise your quality levels, and maintain the momentum of your initiative. To get the best return on your investment, remain competitive, and keep customers content, you need to *sustain the gain*.

So how do you do it? How do you avoid the seemingly inevitable outcome of decreasing momentum and declining participation?

Well, the honest answer is that it's not easy. In fact, it's the hardest thing to do—even harder than learning how to use all the statistical tools! However, it's essential. No matter how difficult it may be, you must strive to keep Six Sigma alive. Otherwise, your customers will eventually feel the negative effects of its disappearance and, therefore, so will you.

There are a few key indicators and guidelines you can put in place to prevent that from happening and to keep the energy level high. That's the purpose of this chapter.

Basic Infrastructure Requirements

If you look at the basic infrastructure required for successful Six Sigma, it's helpful to break it up into a two-year context. In the first year, you lay a foundation for success. In the second year, you follow up on your successful start and build on that foundation.

In the first year, you need to:

- Set up your database for lessons learned.
- Develop your ongoing project list that registers both projected and actual savings.
- Establish your ongoing communication plan, both externally and internally.
- Grow your black belt and green belt resources.
- Create compensation plans and progression plans for a full two years.
- Develop a common metric and reporting/review system that evaluates and updates the status of all projects monthly.

In the second year, you need to:

- Engage your key suppliers in the Six Sigma methodology.
- Build Six Sigma goals into company-wide strategic plans.
- Host quarterly reviews with senior management.
- Host certification events that reward and recognize black belt achievements.
- Develop compensation/incentive plans that include not only black belts and team members but also upper management, to ensure continued support.

- Assign each black belt on four to six projects a year.
- Create a "pull" system for the Six Sigma initiative. Publicize the benefits so widely that you turn away potential black belt candidates because your classes are consistently full.
- Determine the next year's goals for the number of black belts, green belts, master black belts, project selection, and savings projections.

As you make progress with Six Sigma, these elements will become routine and obvious aspects of the overall scope. However, this is where it's most important to recognize that there's no room for complacency or easing off on Six Sigma projects—sustaining their gains is critical to the continual success of your initiative. The items listed above point in one direction: keep Six Sigma focused, keep it moving forward, and keep it in the forefront of everything you do.

Lessons Learned

The first thing you need to do is build and maintain a database of lessons learned. That means documenting what you've learned and achieved with projects to date and then relying on and sharing that information. Once you've fixed something, you need to be able to share what you know about it. It's important to share the lessons far and wide, not only to tout your success, but also to address similar issues elsewhere in the organization. There's not a lot of value in eliminating defects and keeping it to yourself—knowledge transfer needs to happen continually, both inside and outside of the project at hand.

Communication Plan

A communication plan is essential for sharing lessons learned and sustaining your Six Sigma success. Whether it's press releases, monthly newsletters, company intranet updates, video presentations, or quarterly company meetings, you need to get the message out regularly and conspicuously to people inside and outside the organization.

You can report on the progress of projects, itemize dollar savings to date, explain Six Sigma acronyms, or focus on the key tools. What's essential is to continually get the word out on the benefits of Six Sigma.

As you know, all levels of personnel should be familiar with the basics of your Six Sigma mission, including terminology, roles, and metrics. This is to ensure that people can "link" the big picture to actionable items in their own areas. It's all about communicating, in real terms, the powerful implications of each and every project.

Training for Six Sigma

When you start Six Sigma, you focus on training black belts, since they're the tactical leaders of each and every project. What about green belts? Well, when you start out, the ratio of black belts to green belts is about one to three. However, by the time you start the second year, green belts generally increase to about 10% of your company's population.

That increase is based on ever-expanding projects and hands-on expertise, not only by training more candidates for the job. Why? Because the information is shared throughout the organization. As black belts and green belts grow more proficient, they reach out to train others. The exponential benefit is impressive. Your job is to keep the momentum alive by fully exploiting these new resources and assigning them to new projects.

You can take this one step further by requiring that all your staff members be trained as green belts; in this way, you're assured that the majority will not only understand, but also participate in the entire Six Sigma initiative. In fact, this training in and of itself can be a project for black belts as they take on the training responsibility for green belts in their areas.

At least 70% of your black belts should be certified in the first year of your initiative. How are they certified? By completing a minimum of two projects with financial benefits that are independently confirmed by the company controller. (You may remember that in Chapter 4 we discussed the importance of including and informing the controller's department. This becomes even more important when you seek certification.) Black belts also undergo a *tool assessment*, an investigation into whether they're using the tools correctly. The assessment looks at how they interpret the data and whether the maximum financial results from their efforts.

Certification translates to a confirmation that your black belts are doing what they're supposed to, that they're following the DMAIC method and using the key tools to unearth defects and dollars. Black belts also need to show a complete list of backlog projects. Simple as it sounds, if you don't have a list of your backlog projects, you're going to have trouble sustaining the gain. Why? Because it's part of the Six Sigma discipline to document and quantify what you're going to work on, why you're going to work on it, and when. It's essential that this be understood by all.

You need to keep your black belt retention rate high. You want to keep at least 75% of your black belts focused and working on Six Sigma projects. You should aim for a dropout rate of no more than 5% and have a structured plan to replace dropouts. Given the scope of the investment in every aspect, it's critical that you maintain and grow what you've started. Your success in this area can best be measured by filling black belt training classes. Remember that Six Sigma is an ongoing process: you need to keep spreading the message and methodology throughout the organization to retrieve those hidden dollars.

Black Belt Certification Events

Along with certifying black belts, you should formally recognize their accomplishments. As they meet or exceed their individual objectives, you must celebrate their successes along with the company's overall results.

By hosting certification events, you send a clear signal that black belts and their efforts are highly valued. No matter what the individual rank, the project scope, or the dollar value realized, you must demonstrate your appreciation for a job well done. This has ramifications far beyond creating a "feel-good" atmosphere: it shows how seriously you take the Six Sigma work the black belts do and what's in it for those who actively participate.

Company Culture

Linking all your recognition of Six Sigma contributors to the structure of your compensation plans gives you a powerful motivator at the employee level to sustain the gain! Rewarding master black belts, black belts, and green belts for their efforts virtually guarantees sustained interest and energy. You need to establish compensation plans to keep the skill and expertise you've invested so much to develop.

How can you avoid a "brain drain"? Obviously, there's going to be some attrition as people's circumstances change, as they are promoted or leave the company. You can minimize the losses, however, by clearly communicating and committing to a structured, incentive-based compensation plan for all those involved in Six Sigma at any level.

From executives to line workers, from managers to support staff, the compensation plan is a proven tool for keeping the Six Sigma fire burning brightly in the organization. When you "metric" individual performance and tie bonuses to outcomes, you can be assured that your projects will continue to turn in the results you want.

SMART MANAGING

RECOGNITION PAYS

When you publicly acknowledge the successful performance of black belts and their team members, you acknowledge that the investment in Six Sigma has paid off for all parties—company and individuals. Recognition events signal the impact and relevance of Six Sigma projects and indicate just how positive and profitable they are. They certify that black belts have mastered the necessary skills required for eliminating defects in any given process.

Depending on your company size and culture, these certification events can take the form of awards dinners, percentage bonuses, or other incentive packages. They can range from lavish and elaborate occasions to more simple incentive programs, depending on your company culture and size. But whatever the form of recognition, when you emphasize the results achieved, the black belt reward structure speaks to others and inspires them to attain black belt status. Certification events are highly motivating public relations tools that promote each individual success and inspire more successes down the road.

As you look at the progression of your Six Sigma initiative in its first two years of activity, you'll see certain patterns emerge, if you've implemented it correctly. There are certain characteristics to each year's efforts that indicate how well you're sustaining the methodology.

Here's what you want in the first year:

- Train the best of the best for black belt projects.
- Aim for dropout rates under 5%.
- Training Investment should break even within eight months.
- Begin working on backlog of projects and actively manage the reviews.
- Incorporate process metrics and baseline data into strategic plans for the next year.

- Set up a database to track savings and lessons learned.
- Identify two to four master black belts upon completion of training.
- Launch green belt training.

Whether you accomplish all these goals is determined by individual company structures and other real-world issues. However, this list of "signs of success" remains the right place to start. Although this may seem repetitive or obvious to you, it's essential that you put in place structures to monitor your progress right from the start. Otherwise, how can you assess what and how well you are doing?

As you move into your second year as a seasoned Six Sigma expert, here are some additional signs of success:

- Your internal master black belts train new black belts.
- Dollar savings increase by 300% over the first year's target.
- Green belts represent 10% of your company's population.
- All training has transitioned from an outside consultant to your own company resources.
- Communication is ongoing, externally and internally.
- Black belts are being promoted.
- Be sure that project backlog represents no more than 3 to 5% of company revenue.

You may see these comments as wishful thinking when set against your particular reality. But consider the benefits of a self-sustaining and exponential Six Sigma initiative when properly and consistently implemented: you and your company are poised to sustain huge gains and expand them as each year passes. Doing so relies on keeping Six Sigma an active, fully focused part of the company's mission and strategy. If you can work toward that goal and remain committed to fostering the application of Six Sigma in all departments, you'll see the enduring results and return on investment you want.

Company Cycles

Make your suppliers a part of your Six Sigma world. You want them involved in your initiative because, depending on your industry, if you're engaged in making or servicing something, chances are good that you use their parts or processes to complete it. Obviously, they affect your defect levels and waste streams.

Basically, you want to train them and get them up to speed with Six Sigma so they can fix or eliminate defects before they reach you. You can leverage both Six Sigma standards and your supplier relationships to further effective, positive, and lasting change in this area. It's in the best interests of your top 10 suppliers to conform to your new standard of quality—not only to retain your business, but also to improve their own, simply by embracing the core attributes of Six Sigma.

Partnering with suppliers is an excellent source of improvement and savings; by equally sharing in the techniques, tools, and dollar savings, both parties benefit tremendously. Again, it's a long-term view that yields both short- and long-term results. Look into how and where you can do the same with your primary suppliers, because it's an excellent example of how to pick low-hanging fruit.

AGITATING FOR ANSWERS

FOR EXAMPLE I recently consulted with a major appliance manufacturer that had a chronic problem with its washing machines: the agitators routinely did not fit. A one-person task of inserting the agitator often became a two-person job of force-fitting the agitator into the washer. Naturally, customers eventually paid the price for this defect: washing machines that didn't work properly. The cost of poor quality soared when field technicians couldn't fix the problem and had to return the machines to the plant. The cost of this problem amounted to $1 million annually.

The black belt assigned to the problem asked why the agitators sometimes fit and sometimes didn't. He examined all aspects of the part and determined that the weights of the agitators were inconsistent.

It turned out that the supplier had never weighed the agitators! Getting the supplier involved in the project fixed the problem at its source—before the agitators even arrived at the manufacturing plant! The supplier went back through its processes: it examined its 10 injection molds, identified those that were the source of the weight variation, and corrected the problem, so that all agitators were weighted correctly and uniformly.

Everybody in the supply chain won and captured the dollars previously lost in returns, restocking, rework, and the high cost of poor quality that affected them all. Most important, the appliance manufacturer was able to consistently meet customers' expectations of quality.

Reinforcement and Control

It's also necessary for executive management to regularly review and oversee the entire Six Sigma initiative. This is important to reinforce the depth of the Six Sigma commitment and to keep senior leaders involved and engaged in the process. At least quarterly, senior executives should know and understand the progress of all current projects, the financial results achieved, and the projects ahead.

Six Sigma planning should be built into the business plan; it should be considered an integral element of any strategic planning. As goals are set, Six Sigma personnel and projects should be included as key to achieving them. Six Sigma, over time, must become part of the "genetic code" of the business, an integral part of every tactic and strategy. As noted in Chapter 5, it's an executive responsibility to to inspire and promote a Six Sigma culture throughout the organization.

One way to ensure you're sustaining Six Sigma properly is to use a "sustainability checklist" shown below. It's a methodical, clear approach to knowing whether you're managing to keep the fire burning.

THE 21-QUESTION STATUS CHECK

The following 21 questions are an excellent guide to assessing the sustained performance of your Six Sigma initiative. By routinely examining and reinforcing your mission with this status check, you minimize the potential for slipping or slacking in company-wide projects. Keep asking and keep answering these fundamentally important questions and you'll keep your initiative on track:

1. Do you think the Six Sigma process is self-sustaining in your group?
2. What is the status of your master black belts?
3. What is the status of your green belts?
4. How many reviews do your senior executives attend?
5. What are the dropout rates?
6. How many projects are officially completed?
7. How many black belts are ready for certification?
8. Has the finance department been an active part of the process?
9. Have you and the finance department agreed on the guidelines that define true savings?
10. Do you currently have a manual system for tracking the backlog list of black belt projects by plant?
11. Do you have the next set of black belts identified and is upper management supportive?

12. Do you think you are focusing on implementing project completions?
13. Are you attempting to change the program or staying with the black belts' focus?
14. Should you stop doing Six Sigma?
15. What is the status report you are giving to senior management?
16. Are the controllers signing off on your projects?
17. Are the controllers aware of the savings?
18. If you were to spot-check the controllers, what defect rate would you find? (In other words, how many do not know about the savings achieved by the projects?)
19. What database are you going to use through the life of tracking your Six Sigma projects?
20. What is the status of the black belt incentive program discussed at the beginning of the Six Sigma initiative?
21. What are the consequences for champions not helping and driving black belts?

All these questions are highly relevant and thought-provoking. And all your answers must be true and backed up by proof, not assumptions, to keep the momentum going.

The last question is directed at you, specifically, as a manager. You need to honestly examine whether or not you're removing barriers and supporting black belts in their efforts to achieve financial results. If you're not, then you need to take the necessary steps to do so. Remember: black belts and project teams see you as the motivating force, the initiator of the culture change required to identify and remove defects!

Six Sigma is a pervasive and active methodology. Its benefits are too plentiful to relegate it to a sideline role in the vague hope you might get some benefit from it. It works because it's constant and obvious and because it permeates your company. Keeping Six Sigma at the forefront keeps your tangible financial gains at the forefront, too.

The proof that Six Sigma works is its financial impact on the bottom line—you can't misread the dollar savings! Sustaining Six Sigma takes commitment and leadership; you must constantly strive to reinforce its value while introducing it far down the line to other employees. By making sure that your results are broadcast, that your black belt team is solid, and that your executive staff promotes the methodology, you will be well positioned to *sustain the gain*.

Manager's Checklist for Chapter 9

☑ Managers play a key role in sustaining Six Sigma. By developing a database of lessons learned, you can share your findings and techniques for future applications.

☑ Recognize that you must sustain and expand the initial enthusiasm, commitment, and training and the project results you achieve. If you do it right, your results and the momentum will only build! Determine and communicate your expectations for the first and second years of Six Sigma.

☑ Establish and maintain a good communication plan to keep everybody current on your Six Sigma initiative. Use company meetings, newsletters, e-mail, or any other appropriate vehicle to keep awareness high.

☑ Support continual training programs for Six Sigma. Training should take place throughout the organization, both formally and informally. Black belts should train green belts, and you should increase the number of champions and master black belts. Sharing knowledge spreads the Six Sigma message far and wide.

☑ Key to sustaining Six Sigma is to institute a pay-for-performance incentive plan. By linking a bonus structure to project outcomes, you'll maintain the methodology throughout the company.

☑ Host black belt certification events. These are vital for demonstrating the power of the Six Sigma methodology and for recognizing and rewarding a job well done.

☑ Involve your key suppliers in your Six Sigma initiative. Often, some aspect of their product or service may contain a hidden defect that costs you with customers. By partnering to root out defects, you and your supplier both win from the improved productivity.

☑ Be sure senior executives visibly support and endorse Six Sigma with regular reviews. As long as upper management signals that it cares about and believes in the initiative, Six Sigma's strategic importance is clear to all.

☑ Regularly review the Six Sigma sustainability checklist. This is an excellent tool for measuring the health of your initiative over time.

Six Sigma
Proof Positive

There is one rule for industrialists and that is: Make the best quality
of goods possible at the lowest cost possible, paying the highest
wages possible.

—Henry Ford (1863-1947)

So, now that you've read about the basic how-tos of Six Sigma, what
do you think? Is it possible to deliver the best quality goods at the
lowest cost *and* compensate people fairly? Once again, the answer
is a resounding yes—if you implement Six Sigma and maintain it over
time to get those results.

It's a simple enough formula: give your customers what they want,
when they want it, at a competitive price—their CTQ factors—and your
company can emerge as the highest-quality, lowest-cost provider. At the
same time, retaining people in whom you've invested time and training is
essential, and that's best accomplished by compensating and rewarding
them with wages and bonuses that truly reflect their high value. When
you do this, you demonstrate your level of commitment to making it work
by sending the clear message that you want results and that you'll do
what it takes to get them. It shows your employees that your commitment
isn't theoretical. By lobbying for and getting them competitive compensation, you're telling them that you mean business, that you're committing to supporting their satisfaction as they're committed to the satisfing
customers by deploying Six Sigma full time, front and center.

Where's the downside? There isn't one—everyone's CTQ factors are being met and sustained. As automobile giant Henry Ford said, highest-quality, lowest-cost products delivered by well-paid employees is the single most important business rule of all—and it's a rule that will yield continual results. In all the definitions, phases, project selection, statistical tools, and personnel training issues you've read about here, the Six Sigma bottom line is to make sure your bottom line continues to grow—to return hidden revenue to the balance sheet and boost your productivity at every level.

OK, so you know this by now. After all, it's the main theme of this book and the central message of Six Sigma. "Where's the proof?" I can imagine you saying. Well, that's what you'll see in this chapter.

I'm going to show you the proof, with final reports and real case studies, and give you actual examples of how to recruit, train, and retain quality personnel to serve as black belts and green belts. There's also a section on champion training and definitions that pertains to you in your managerial capacity. While this may seem repetitive, it really isn't, because the information in this chapter can serve as your template for launching your own initiative. Further, from the case studies to each job description and on to the next level of Six Sigma, you'll see all the information you've read about in the preceding chapters come together coherently and effectively. It's proof positive that Six Sigma works.

Real Final Reports

Once you've defined your project, the team's been trained, the metrics are in place, the team has used the DMAIC method, and the results are in—then what? Well, that's when you and your black belts sit down and compile all you've learned into a final report.

That final report is more than a summary of your project activities or an accounting of expenses incurred. It's a comprehensive statement of work and a reference tool for future projects. It thoroughly examines each project objective and the steps taken. It delivers an overview that plots the process and indicates where the defects were found, what statistical tools were used to identify them, how the black belt determined corrective action, and the resulting savings.

To be effective, final reports need to include certain elements that present and quantify a given project's objectives. While each one is unique to the problem addressed, there are seven basic sections that you need to incorporate in each report. Within each, you can get as specific as necessary about a

FINAL REPORT FACTS   SMART

Each final report becomes a milestone on your Six Sigma road map. They are invaluable resources for indicating the MANAGING sequential nature of projects and why it's necessary to proceed that way. Remember: avoid the opinions and stick to the data. Final reports present the facts and the process that fixed the defects in a disciplined, logical sequence.

given project in terms of how you went about measuring, analyzing, improving, and controlling the problem. To review what we discussed in Chapter 8, there are the seven main sections to develop:

1. Executive Summary
   1.1 Main Problem
   1.2 Project Goals
   1.3 Project Results

2. Problem Statement
   2.1 Customer Requirements
   2.2 Project Objectives
   2.3 Outline of Project Strategy
   2.4 Project Schedule
   2.5 Final Project Description

3. Experimental Data (actions taken)
   3.1 Gauge Studies
   3.2 Materials Characterization (if appropriate)
   3.3 Process Specifications
   3.4 Capability Studies (short- and long-term)
   3.5 Design of Experiments

4. Implementation
   4.1 Operating Specification
   4.2 Process FMEA
   4.3 Performance Tracking Systems

Since all projects are not created equal, each final report must address the unique concerns and conclusions of each within these main sections and their subsections. (This is where you get to demonstrate your competence with the statistical tools you learned about in Chapter 7.) The main headings are a place to start understanding the basics of a final report. As you conduct each project, you write up the critical information that you and the project team have gathered to justify the project's goals and demonstrate how and why you reached your conclusions.

Case Studies

To understand better how the theoretical is transformed into real-world application, how you can deploy Six Sigma to drive down defects and drive up profitability, it helps to examine actual Six Sigma projects. Even though this book has presented and discussed the method, tools, personnel, and other project management aspects, it's valuable to take a look at individual projects across the spectrum of industries to get a sense of the methodology in action. Once you take a good look at these case studies, you'll also see how their progression and functions are mirrored by the sequence and detail of the final reports discussed. These case studies give you an insight into how valuable a final report is, both to illustrate the project just concluded and to serve as a case study for future project teams.

Case Study #1: Fulfilling Government Orders

A company that counts a large government agency as one of its customers repeatedly experienced some significant cash flow and receivables problems associated with this account. The company (we'll call it

Company X) needed to unplug this bottleneck to improve cash flow and better manage receivables.

The Main Issue. A government customer issued a significant number of unpriced orders for specialized products. Because of Company X's long administrative time frames, it often shipped these products to the customer before the company and the agency had agreed on prices for the products. This practice meant Company X experienced a constant level of $13 million in nominal receivables for these orders, which reduced its cash flow and directly cost up to $400,000 in tied-up capital.

The Project. The goal of this Six Sigma project was to reduce by 85% the total receivables trapped due to unpriced orders.

The Strategy. The black belt and his project team went to work using the MAIC method and deploying statistical tools within each project phase to determine where and how the bottlenecks were occurring. They mapped the existing process, then developed an alternative process to correct the variations within it.

"M" is for Measure. The team introduced measurements into the order issue, entry, scheduling, proposal, and negotiation phases of the process, using the existing management information system to flag out-of-control phases against what they should be according to specifications.

"A" is for Analyze. The team set targets for order processing times for each phase of the order process. Charts monitored performance at each stage, and out-of-control exceptions were noted and investigated.

"I" is for Improve. Once the measurements and analysis were complete, the black belt had the data he needed to approach the customer and resolve the consequence of unpriced orders. Those negotiations resulted in Company X's ability to bill 75% of the proposed value of the order at the time of shipment. A tracking report for unpriced orders was introduced, and Company X adopted first in, first out (FIFO) order processing.

"C" is for Control. Permanent changes were introduced into Company X's MIS system to handle and monitor unpriced orders. As a result of this project, further work is anticipated in the overall order entry process. Additionally, the customer and the company are working to reduce the use of unpriced orders.

The Results. The black belt and his team reduced the amount of receivables trapped by unpriced orders by 96%, well in excess of their original 85% target. This freed up $12.5 million during the four months of the project's duration. The company saved $300,000 to 400,000 per year in financing charges.

Case Study #2: Scrapping Defects in Manufacturing

Managers at a manufacturing company that we'll call Company Y were aware that certain defects in a component were resulting in a lot of scrap, which caused a money drain.

The Main Issue. On a particular high-speed rotating component, the size and location of an oil drain slot determined the service life of the component, due to the stresses induced. Since the slot was inadequately manufactured, the annual known costs of scrap from it amounted to $170,000.

The Project Goal. The black belt assigned to this situation recognized that the primary goal was to identify and eliminate the inconsistent manufacturing processes that were causing all the scrap and rework. Once she had done that, she could then drive the dollar savings out of these waste streams and into the bottom line. At a minimum, her goal was to save the identified $170,000.

"M" is for Measure. The black belt and her team conducted a gauge R&R (repeatability and reproducibility) study that showed the existing measuring system variation contributed to 17.5% of the total variation as measured on the smallest dimension. Although that was greater than the preferred 10%, it was still less than the recommended maximum of 30%. Measurements of the oil slot dimensions indicated a short sigma value, ranging from 0.6 (forward slot axial position) to 65.8 (aft slot parallelism). The black belt and her team worked to identify reasons for the low sigma values.

"A" is for Analyze. A tooling pin that established the component's alignment in the machining fixture was identified as having a significant run-out (taper) that placed the component in an out-of-specification location of the component in the fixture. Additionally, the pin holder was found to be damaged. It was replaced immediately and the axial location sigma values rose to 4.3 from 0.6. By using hypothesis testing, the team identified tool deflection and tool as the major causes of deviation from the requirements.

"I" is for Improve. The black belt suggested that a stiffer tool holder be introduced, together with a scheduled program of regular mill tool changes. She then proposed enlarging and changing the slot profile so that a larger milling tool could be introduced that would deflect less during use. Following that, the team conducted a simulation study on the impact of the life expectancy for the component with the enlarged slot.

"C" is for Control. A trial slot design was analyzed, together with a complete three-dimensional stress analysis, to determine the impact of the change. Changes were made to setups and manufacturing, and a further risk analysis was undertaken upon introducing the new slot design.

The Results. The final throughput yield increased from 28% to 94% for the finished component with the existing slot design, which amounted to nearly double the projected savings, or $309,000 annually.

Case Study #3: Accounting for Delinquent Accounts

Welcome to Company Z, where delinquent customer accounts more than 30 days overdue are costing the company at least $7 million per month!

The Main Issue. Approximately 65% of these overdue accounts resulted from commercial issues or administrative problems. At current commercial interest rates, this represented a $325,000 annual expense to Company Z, which it could ill afford.

The Project Strategy. The black belt and his team needed to identify why, where, and how these accounts were becoming overdue and how to change processes to avoid the staggering cost of errors in this transactional environment.

"M" is for Measure. The black belt started by developing primary and secondary metrics to track the progress of this project. First, he categorized monthly delinquent accounts receivable dollars that were less than 30 days overdue, with a baseline of $7 million per month. Then he segmented the monthly delinquent accounts receivable dollars by total month-end accounts with the assumption that 15% were defective. Process maps and interviews were conducted with all personnel throughout each functional area. A new measuring system was installed to assign category and causes to receivable disputes as well as a two-level Pareto analysis of the previous 12 months of disputes. They identified four issues that contributed to 80% of the commercial disputes, which in turn contributed to 65% of all delinquent accounts.

"A" is for Analyze. The team obtained additional order data by salesperson, district, region, order type, etc. Hypothesis tests showed no significant difference among the groups. But a cause-and-effect matrix and an FMEA isolated a list of five factors (Xs) that were found to drive those four issues. All five factors (Xs) resulted in sales order information that was inconsistent with purchase order/contract information.

"I" is for Improve. The black belt team conducted a designed experiment at the order point to validate these five factors. As a result, a new corporate policy, IT procedures, and a training program were initiated.

"C" is for Control. To ensure that the gains were sustained, the black belt instituted a time series analysis and other monitoring devices that would flag any new deviations from or backsliding into old process patterns.

The Results. Company Z stopped the financial drain on its resources and greatly improved its cash flow. It saved $325,000 annually and had reliable mechanisms in place to ensure that over time it wouldn't end up where it was before Six Sigma.

Essential Elements of Six Sigma Success

These case studies have one thing in common—dedicated, well-trained black belt teams along with support structures that rewarded and championed the team efforts to get the results the companies needed. This is another instance that takes us back to an essential ingredient of Six Sigma success—fully trained, fully supported black belts who are free to use what they know to locate and eliminate defects. Your projects—from selection to final report—depend on the people you assign to work on them and the ways in which you reward them. Choose your people well and reward them generously; you'll be astounded at the energy, enthusiasm, and end results you generate.

Training Agendas

So now we get into some training and job description issues for your project teams. At this point, you may well be thinking, "Haven't we already gone over this before?" Well, yes, we have. But this is a message that not only bears repeating, but also deserves further definition to give you the most comprehensive understanding of what is involved in training Six Sigma operatives—not only black belts and green belts—but you in your role as champion.

An educated and informed champion is in an excellent position to select and direct key staff members as black belts. Black belt training is extensive, if not exhaustive. You need to be prepared to facilitate and encourage that process to graduate a black belts who have the expertise to deliver on the investment made in their training.

It's important to reiterate that a black belt is not a part-time role. The time and investment it takes to fully train and equip black belts would never see a return if they did not go to work at Six Sigma full time. Black belts are the catalysts driving the change—they need to have all the infor-

---

CHAMPIONING YOUR ROLE

SMART

MANAGING

You already know what the champion does in his or her role in Six Sigma, but you might not be aware of basic training elements that determine how well equipped a person is for the task. You're far more than a cheerleader or magician who makes barriers disappear. At a minimum, a champion must be trained in the following:

- Project selection methods
- Basic statistics
- Capability analysis
- Measurement systems analysis
- Process mapping
- XY matrix
- Hypothesis testing
- Design of experiments

If you know what your black belts are doing, you can better understand all their findings in their final reports and, in turn, present and explain those results to upper management. It's essential that you be well versed in all the tools and methodologies of Six Sigma so you can be a smart and effective champion.

mation and tools at their disposal to make decisions, plot projects, and
dig out variation wherever it exists.

Training for black belts basically follows the DMAIC sequence. They
learn about measuring, analyzing, improving, and controlling processes
in intensive, hands-on training sessions that take eight hours a day, five
days a week, for a month—30 days of nonstop immersion in learning
what makes Six Sigma tick.

> **CAUTION**
> ### NO SHORTCUTS TO BLACK BELT TRAINING
> There are no shortcuts to black belt training. Both you and
> your candidates need to know and accept this going in. Each
> session is extensive, interactive, and time-consuming. You cannot
> skip any aspect of it and think you've got what it takes to imple-
> ment Six Sigma. Like everything else in the methodology, training is sequen-
> tial and builds on necessary steps. You can't hurry the process. But then,
> with that Six Sigma training, well-armed black belts will rapidly transform
> the organization wherever they apply their skills and knowledge.

Here's a look at what black belt training agendas entail:

Session One: Measure. Black belts are introduced to Six Sigma; assigned
projects; taught process mapping, FMEA matrices, statistics, capability
studies, measurement systems, and project application; and given regular homework.

Session Two: Analyze. Black belts learn how to analyze distributions,
graphically plot data, do hypothesis testing, and plan project applications
while completing regular homework assignments.

Session Three: Improve. By week three, black belts are ready to learn the
Design of Experiments method, understand correlation studies, conduct
full factorial experiments, and then plan and execute project plans.

Session Four: Control. Digging into all the control tools, black belts now
enter the final phase of training by reviewing the methodology, learning
how to implement statistical methods of control and mistake proofing,
and finalizing their project work.

This is where it all comes together—black belts have the tools, know
how to use them, and are ready for you to champion their cause as they
take on projects.

In addition, the green belts receive training in the methodology so they can assist and support the black belts. Without a working knowledge of the methodology, they would be severely limited in the kinds of assistance and support they could provide. Their training is not as rigorous or detailed as that of the black belts, but green belts receive guidance to increase their technical knowledge to the point that they become local experts at solving problems—which creates another path to bottom-line savings.

Job Descriptions

As stated earlier, being a champion or a black belt is not a part-time job. All the training and discipline just considered would be a waste of time and money if the champions and black belts didn't put it to use right away. These are full-time jobs and must be recognized that way by the company. To that end, you need job descriptions to define the positions of champion and black belt to elicit interest from potential candidates.

Like any other job description common in business today, these descriptions should indicate the title, level, reporting structure, purpose, responsibilities, and qualifications required. By developing a standardized job description, you further indicate the permanent, full-time character of Six Sigma.

The following examples of Six Sigma job postings should give you a good idea of what to include.

OPEN POSITION NOTICE

Position Title: Champion
Organization Level:
Business Unit or Organization:
Location of Job:
Position Reports to (Immediate Supervisor): VP level or higher

Position Purpose: The customers that form the enormous base of today's world market are sending a clear and undeniable message: produce higher-quality products at lower cost with greater responsiveness. Numerous companies have heard this message and are rising to the Six Sigma challenge. For many, Six Sigma has led to breakthrough improvement of business, engineering, manufacturing, service, and administrative processes. Such a process-oriented focus leads to significant reductions in cost and cycle time; however, the principal focus is always on the continuous improvement of customer satisfaction. To this end, the Six Sigma champion certification program was conceived, designed, and developed. The intent of this program is to provide key individuals with the managerial and technical knowledge necessary to facilitate the leadership, implementation, and deployment of Six Sigma. The instructional goal is to teach and reinforce fundamental Six Sigma strategies, tactics, and tools necessary for achieving breakthroughs in key product designs, manufacturing processes, services, and administrative processes. To support this focus, program delivery has been structured into two self-contained segments that, when successfully completed, lead to certification. The resulting certificate denotes and communicates a high level of executive commitment, dedication, competency, and leadership.

Qualifications (skills or talents) that a candidate *must* possess to gain consideration for this position: Prior success in leading a team and key individuals to a business result. Demonstrated project management skills. Technical competence in basic statistical calculations and graphical analysis such as Pareto, time series, and correlation. Basic knowledge of concepts of problem solving and coaching employees. Proven track record in removing barriers and dealing directly with organizational issues to resolve conflict between and within functional groups. Demonstrates leadership through actions and follow-up. Proficient in basic budget and accounting principles within business units and between functional boundaries.

Additional desirable qualifications that will be important in making the final candidate selection: Managerial and technical knowledge necessary to facilitate the leadership, implementation, and deployment of Six Sigma. Ability to understand basic Six Sigma concepts and fit them into realistic implementation action plans. Understands and practices business planning that links to company strategies. Ability to mentor and inspire key individuals and teams to reach new levels of improvement. A relentless desire to improve the current state of the business. A respected leader inside the company. This position is ideally suited for the person who is given the task of implementing new projects or initiatives in the company with a proven track record of successful results.

OPEN POSITION NOTICE

Position Title: Black Belt

Organization Level:

Business Unit or Organization:

Location of Job:

Position Reports to (Immediate Supervisor): Champion and Project Leadership

Position Purpose: Black belts are contributors from various disciplines who, when trained, become change agents for operational excellence. Black belts have earned a high level of peer respect and are clearly seen as leaders—they manage risks, set direction, and lead the way to breakthrough improvement. They are paradigm shifters who help others discover a better improvement process. They should be encouraged to stimulate management thinking by posing new ways of doing things, to challenge conventional wisdom by demonstrating successful application of new methodologies, to seek out and pilot new tools, to create innovative thinking, and to serve as role models for others who follow in their footsteps.

Qualifications (skills or talents) that a candidate *must* possess to gain consideration for this position: Process/product knowledge, basic statistical knowledge, organizational knowledge, and communication skills. Able to perform work of analytical, detailed, and logical nature. Must have demonstrated project management skills. Must have a detailed understanding of customer requirements and understand basic business practices.

Additional qualifications that will be important in making the final candidate selection: Be a self-starter who is open-minded, goal-oriented, and willing to learn, with a desire to drive change and improve current standards and is a team player. Basic statistical knowledge. Must learn advance quality planning, FMEA, and statistical process control. Actively advocate on behalf of project teams. Demonstrate high energy and trustworthiness.

Job descriptions are a good way to ensure that your candidates possess necessary qualifications and help you eliminate unqualified candidates or those with only a superficial interest. This is crucial when you consider the time and resources it takes to train black belts; you want to be as sure as possible that you'll invest in someone with the credentials and motivation to succeed in the long term.

Design for Six Sigma

Looking into the future, the goal is to obtain the maximum return on your Six Sigma investment by spreading it throughout your company, growing the black belt population, and sustaining the exponential gains you achieve by keeping the Six Sigma process going.

In addition to the expanding practice of Six Sigma and driving more dollars to the bottom line, there's another dimension to consider. Six Sigma doesn't exist in a vacuum. While its principles remain constant, there's an evolution of its message that can take companies in exciting new directions. I'm referring to the discipline known as Design for Six Sigma (DFSS).

> **Design for Six Sigma (DFSS)** A systematic methodology that uses tools, training, and measurements to enable the design of products, services, and processes that meet customer expectations at Six Sigma quality levels. DFSS optimizes the design process to achieve Six Sigma performance and integrates Six Sigma practices at the outset of new product development with a disciplined set of tools.
>
> **KEY TERM**

Robert G. Cooper states in *Winning at New Products: Accelerating the Process from Idea to Launch* (Perseus Books, 2001, 3rd edition) that only about 60% of new products succeed and that for every seven new product ideas, only four make it to development, and just one succeeds. What's wrong with this picture? The new product cycle is definitely not operating at a six-sigma level. In fact, it's closer to the average four-sigma quality level at which many companies operate today. Plus, even as manufacturing problems are corrected by deploying Six Sigma methods, newly developed products often are the source of new problems. So, an organization practicing the methodology in various functional areas and attaining Six Sigma status may be far below that in developing new products or services.

Once you've mastered the essentials of Six Sigma, you may be ready for the essentials of DFSS, to carry that improvement into the development and design of your new products. DFSS is based on the idea that when you design Six Sigma quality into the new product development process, it's probable that you'll sustain that gain too as customers accept that item. By incorporating DFSS, you're virtually assured that the product or service you're launching will perform dependably in the marketplace, thus setting it up for customer acceptance. Like its parent Six Sigma initiative, DFSS uses a disciplined set of tools to bring high quality to launches.

DFSS begins by conducting a gap analysis of your entire product development system. A gap analysis identifies the gaps in your processes that negatively affect new product performance. DFSS also addresses another significant factor, the voice of the customer. Every new product decision must be driven by the VOC; otherwise, what basis do you have for introducing the product? By learning how to identify that voice and responding to it, you're in a far better position to deliver a new product or service that customers actually want.

Once the gap analysis is done and the VOC is identified, DFSS goes to work with its own version of DMAIC, using a five-step process:

1. **Plan.** Enables the team to succeed with the project by mapping all vital steps.
2. **Identify.** Hears the voice of the customer that guides you to select the best product concept.
3. **Design.** Builds a thorough knowledge base about the product and its processes.
4. **Optimize.** Achieves balance of quality, cost, and time to market.
5. **Validate.** Demonstrates that the VOC has been heard and satisfied.

(Some Six Sigma people equate DFSS with another five-step process—DMADV: define, measure, analyze, design, and verify. Others use only four steps—IDOV. Design for Six Sigma is a relatively new concept, so we must expect some inconsistencies and evolution of the models as companies and consultants apply them.)

Once again, the success of this Six Sigma offshoot requires active management participation. You and upper management must monitor its progress regularly to keep it on course. DFSS can be a useful tool to companies as they get comfortable with Six Sigma and look to grow its benefits in other areas.

Ultimately, DFSS is not that different from the Six Sigma work you're undertaking. In fact, it's a natural progression to continually—and relentlessly—root out defects and direct hidden dollars to the bottom line.

The End ... and the Beginning

In conclusion, let me say that I recognize that for you to grasp all the concepts presented in this book is like trying to drink from the proverbial fire hose. There's a lot to learn about Six Sigma, more than I could cover in these pages. It's not an easy task to undertake and it's a continually evolving lesson in quality improvement. But, to return to a theme that has permeated this book, in order for you to fully "get" Six Sigma, you have to dive in and practice it. Although I've broken it down and attempted to illustrate it as simply as possible, these pages are only theory to you. When you take the plunge and put Six Sigma into action, the light will come on, and you'll be able to say, "Now I get it!"

If you get anything at all from this book, I hope it's these two things:

- The Six Sigma journey is a full-time trip and never, ever ends, as long as you want to attain the pinnacle of quality and grow the bottom line in your role as the highest-quality, lowest-cost producer of goods and services.
- To sustain the Six Sigma gain and create a Six Sigma culture, middle managers must be relentless in the pursuit of this journey by setting it as a priority in their business plans.

After all, as Henry Ford said all those years ago, it's the one rule by which to conduct a successful business. It's simple. It's Six Sigma.

Manager's Checklist for Chapter 10

☑ Managers need to be sure that comprehensive final reports are assembled for each completed project. By doing so, you create a record of the procedures and processes involved in a specific project that can serve as a template for future projects.

☑ It's helpful to consider real-world case studies of Six Sigma projects. When you recognize just how flexible and valuable the methodology is across many functions, you'll appreciate how you can adapt it to your needs.

☑ How you obtain training for yourself and your teams in Six Sigma is important. It's essential that you as a champion understand the tools and techniques black belts use. It's equally important that black belts fully understand these tools to do their jobs.

☑ Knowing the professional responsibilities of both champions and black belts further defines these roles and credentials. Specific, sequential, and thorough training programs are necessary to gain that knowledge.

☑ Once you have your Six Sigma initiative well under way with existing processes, the next logical step is to examine your new product and/or service development functions. An extension of the methodology, Design for Six Sigma, helps you improve and control product launches by designing Six Sigma quality right into your development processes.

Index